FAST
TRACK

FAST
TRACK

Training and Nutrition Secrets
from America's Top Female Runner

by **SUZY FAVOR HAMILTON** and **JOSE ANTONIO, Ph.D.**

RODALE

Notice
The information in this book is meant to supplement, not replace, proper exercise training. All forms of exercise pose some inherent risks. The editors and publisher advise readers to take full responsibility for their safety and know their limits. Before practicing the exercises in this book, be sure that your equipment is well-maintained, and do not take risks beyond your level of experience, aptitude, training, and fitness. The exercise and dietary programs in this book are not intended as a substitute for any exercise routine or dietary regimen that may have been prescribed by your doctor. As with all exercise and dietary programs, you should get your doctor's approval before beginning.

Mention of specific companies, organizations, or authorities in this book does not imply endorsement by the author or publisher, nor does mention of specific companies, organizations, or authorities imply that they endorse this book, its author, or the publisher.

Internet addresses and telephone numbers given in this book were accurate at the time it went to press.

Printed in the United States of America
Rodale Inc. makes every effort to use acid-free (∞), recycled paper (♻) .

Book design by Chris Rhoads

Library of Congress Cataloging-in-Publication Data

Favor Hamilton, Suzy.
  Fast track : training and nutrition secrets from America's top female runner / Suzy Favor Hamilton and Jose Antonio, Ph.D.
      p.   cm.
  Includes bibliographical references and index.
  ISBN 1–59486–013–0 paperback
  1. Runners (Sports)—Nutrition. 2. Athletes—Nutrition. 3. Cookery. I. Antonio, Jose, Ph.D. II. Title.
  TX361.R86F38   2004
  613.2'024'79642—dc22   2004007766

Distributed to the trade by Holtzbrinck Publishers

  6 8 10 9 7 5   paperback

To my twin daughters, Brooke and Brandi Antonio,
in whom I hope to instill the value of physical fitness
—Jose Antonio, Ph.D.

To all the young female runners out there
who aspire to reach their potential
—Suzy Favor Hamilton

Contents

CONTENTS

CONTENTS

Acknowledgments

We'd like to thank Cami Wells for her insight on training programs and Dr. Chris Lydon for edifying us on the subject of the Female Athlete Triad.

A special thanks (from Jose) to my wife and kids for the endless hours watching me stare at my computer screen wondering when this book project would be completed.

Also a special thanks (from Suzy) to my coach, Peter Tegen, for the wonderful workouts, to my therapist, Gerard Hartmann, for keeping me going, and to my husband, Mark, for providing knowledge, support, and love.

And we'd especially like to thank Lou Schuler for believing in this book project!

Experience Is the Greatest Teacher

CHAPTER 1

Suzy's Personal Epiphany
six lessons I've learned
the hard way

Let me get this straight right off the bat—even professional runners make mistakes. Yes, myself included. Although I ran well and experienced much success in high school and college, I look back on those early days and cringe. I could have run so much better. I could have been healthier, too, if only I had the knowledge.

I like to think I'm a good example of someone who made many of the common mistakes of a young female runner, but came out of it okay. In the long run, I was lucky to be able to correct most of my mistakes quickly enough to avoid irreparable damage.

I've spent the past several years at the Foot Locker National High School Cross-Country Championships watching young running talent and spending time with the young ladies who compete there. As you may know, I participated in these championships years ago, so I see myself in so many of these young women. They are truly talented, exceptional young people. And this is why it pains me when I see young girls making the same types of mistakes that I made in my day.

The most prominent problems include eating disorders, overtraining, and lack of knowledge when it comes to diet and training—the same kinds of problems that I experienced when I was younger. Spending time at the championships with so many amazing young athletes reminded me of my past mistakes and motivated me to put together this book you're holding right now. What kind of lessons have I learned throughout my career? Here are six of the most important ones.

lesson #1: eat more, run better

When I was a senior in high school, people around me had figured out that I had some running talent. I had experienced success throughout my first 3 years in high school, with several state titles, but along with that success came expectations for me to do bigger and better things. I lived in a small town, so I was constantly mentioned in the local newspaper and pictured on the TV news. I had high expectations for myself and wanted to be the best. I felt the pressure and understood fully that others expected me to succeed.

When I went to the Kinney Meet (now the Foot Locker Cross-Country Championships) during my junior year, I saw other successful runners my age who were thinner, and in some cases, faster than I was. It didn't take long for me to notice that being lighter meant being faster. I wanted so badly to be thin like them so that I could run faster. So, during my senior year, I consciously tried to eat less. I was 5 feet 4 inches and 106 pounds, and saw myself as big, simply because I was around girls who were bone thin. I didn't realize at the time that I was actually at my ideal weight.

Fortunately, I couldn't stick to my dieting regimen. I'd get too hungry, so I never reached that ultra-thin dangerous state. Nonetheless, I still wasn't eating enough, considering the calories I was burning during the day, and I wasn't eating the right foods. When I ate, it was junk food, pizza, a Pop-Tart—you know, not exactly the types of food elite athletes should be eating. As a result, I became undernourished and my body lacked the nutrients essential to my health as both a young girl and a runner. Of course, improper nutrition was just the first of my problems.

lesson #2: a proper diet helps prevent injuries
My nutrition issues didn't disappear when I entered college. In college, my running volume and intensity increased, yet my nutrition regimen was still as terrible as always. In particular, I wasn't consuming enough calcium. Consequently, in January of my freshman year, right before my indoor track season was to start, I was diagnosed with a stress fracture in my femur that sidelined me for 6 weeks. The doctor hinted that my injury could stem from a lack of nourishment.

He was right. My nutrition was so poor that my bones weren't as strong as they should have been. Thankfully, around the same time I was diagnosed with the stress fracture, I started dating my future husband. He noticed my poor eating habits almost immediately and soon began to nag me about eating better. He couldn't believe how little I ate considering how much I worked out. At the time, I was trying to eat less to make up for the lack of intense training because of my injury. I worried that eating any more would cause me to put on weight. Mark encouraged me to eat more, which is what I needed to hear. I wanted to please him so much, so I started eating properly and even enrolled in a nutrition class at school.

My eating certainly didn't go from terrible to perfect overnight. That nutrition class helped me make some important changes, but it has taken me years to finally get things right.

I consider myself one of the lucky ones. Although I had a distorted view of my body and weight and didn't eat properly, I never got to the point of being anorexic. Over the years, I've seen so many runners de-

---

Before and After Here's an example of what I used to eat during a typical day in college compared with a typical day now.

MY COLLEGE DIET
Breakfast: Orange juice, Cheerios, a Pop-Tart
Lunch: Slice of pizza and a cola
Dinner: Spaghetti and fruit punch
Snack: Popcorn or chips

MY CURRENT DIET
Breakfast: Oatmeal with 30 grams of protein powder mixed in, a slice of turkey bacon, yogurt, and glass of mineral water
Snack: Protein bar or shake
Lunch: 2 chicken tacos and a protein smoothie
Snack: Rice cake with honey and half a protein shake
Dinner: Steak stir-fry with brown rice and a chocolate-chip cookie
Snack: Slow-acting, casein-based protein drink

---

stroy themselves and their careers as they teeter on the brink of anorexia. The reduced weight may lead them to faster running initially, but after a while, they really start to struggle. Injuries pop up left and right, and their bodies begin to break down. It never fails. Most of them start performing so badly, they just quit. I wish I could have known at an early age how important it is to consume enough protein, calcium, and other essential vitamins, but at least I learned and was able to adjust. It isn't easy to start over once the downward spiral has started. The ironic thing is that when young runners don't eat enough, they screw up their metabolism so badly that many times they end up becoming quite heavy when (and if) they're able to overcome anorexia.

lesson #3: fast food doesn't create fast runners Sophomore year brought

more bad news from the doctor. My cross-country season had been a disappointment. I was 2nd at the NCAA Cross-Country Championships my freshman year, but had fallen to 26th the following season. I didn't know what was wrong with me. My coach, perplexed, suggested I get checked out. I had never had my blood checked, so it was a bit of a shock when I was told that I had anemia (a lack of iron in the blood). Again, my diet undoubtedly was the root cause of this condition, because I ate almost all carbohydrates and rarely any meat (one of the highest food sources of iron).

Throughout my running career, I had this entrenched belief that I shouldn't eat anything for at least 3 to 4 hours before my workout or race. I was fearful of getting cramps or feeling too full to run. Looking back on those races now, I remember that many of my extremely intense races and workouts ended in disaster. Many times I would feel lousy or even collapse at the end of my workout. Today, I realize it all stemmed from poor nutrition.

When I was in college, winning nine NCAA championships, I ate most of my meals at Rocky Rococo (a pizza joint) and Kentucky Fried Chicken. At my apartment, the usual fare was Kraft Macaroni and Cheese or spaghetti. I ate a ton of toast. Admittedly, I just loved junk food. Although I had already learned that I needed to put food in my tank to perform well, I was still learning exactly which foods to put in at which times. I simply didn't understand how important food was to my performance. I justified consuming this junk food by thinking that I was working it off. And although I was, I now realize that I could have been leaner (not necessarily thinner, but fitter) and more prepared for workouts and races. I still recall feeling sluggish at many a workout and race. Now I know why. I can remember a nutritionist coming one day before practice to speak to our team about foods, but she just kind of explained the four food groups and went home. I probably didn't pay too much attention either.

My poor eating habits can probably be traced back to growing up in Wisconsin. There, typical meals consist of bratwurst, fried fish, and beer. I wasn't exactly surrounded by a bunch of health nuts (you should see the looks I get from waitresses these days when I ask for a *plain* chicken sandwich). Hopefully, you can understand why I developed my junk food habits and why those around me weren't trying to correct them at the time. It just isn't easy to eat right, especially in college, when you're often in a hurry and running on a limited budget. Dorm food is full of starches. It's all pasta and bread, pasta and bread!

As recently as 1997, I still had little clue about foods and their effect on performance. At the World Championships in Athens, I was downing 3 to 4 glasses of cola every day. This practice was not only giving me several hundred additional calories I didn't need but also taking me on a roller coaster ride where my energy levels would go up and down. When it came time to compete, I lacked the energy I needed. I know it sounds amazing that someone at my level would have no clue about something so essential, but if you aren't informed, what can you do?

lesson #4: rest days are vital to success
Back in high school and college I never took a day off. If I did, I thought my competition would get ahead of me. We've all felt that way, right? I think that's a good belief to have if you're going to be the best. But it's even more important to realize that quality of rest is just as important as quality of training.

Simply put, when your body is telling you to chill, you need to chill. People think you need to train hard all the time, but that just isn't true. It takes a strong, smart athlete to set aside time for rest. I found this out firsthand.

In summer 2002, I spent 2 months in Europe racing, and had my best season ever. I believe a big reason for the success was that I didn't overtrain and had a great deal of recovery time in between weekly races. I had put in the hard work leading up to these races, so my workouts during this period were not terribly intense. The quality was good, but the quantity was minimal. People don't believe me when I tell them that I put in only about five hard workouts in the 2 months I was over there. But it's true. Recovery during the summer season is a must because you're racing every weekend with the best in the world. You need to be sharp every time, and to be sharp, you need to be rested. My coach's philosophy was "when in doubt, be conservative."

Here's another example of the importance of rest. A former competitor of mine was not racing well 2 weeks before the Olympic Trials in 1992. She claimed that she was tired and worn out. Her coach had her take a full week off from running and a week later, she made the Olympic team. Believe me, you aren't going to lose fitness with a little bit of rest here and there. If you're feeling sluggish or need to give an injury a break, don't be afraid to take some time off. I find myself constantly taking days off, at least a couple a month. I also mix light training days into my schedule to allow myself to recover, in preparation for the intense workouts and races I face throughout the season.

lesson #5: cross-training will keep you healthy

Fortunately, injuries weren't a huge problem for me back in high school and college, but they did pop up on occasion. I remember feeling aches and pains and being afraid to tell my college coach. He didn't want sissy runners, so I didn't complain. I saw a lot of teammates do the same thing, and, sadly, some of those little aches and pains turned into serious injuries.

Back then, cross-training really wasn't an option. For some reason, many of the athletes and coaches around me didn't believe that cross-training was as effective as running. Today, I know better and cross-train 2 to 3 days a week. I still run nearly every day, but I like to mix things up, too. For example, if I have a 70-minute run planned but find myself feeling achy, I might change it to a 40-minute run and then hop on the stationary bike or into the pool for 30 minutes instead. Cross-training works and is essential. Trust me, those miles on the pavement come back to haunt you eventually. You just don't see it coming when you're young because you feel invincible.

I can remember back in high school when I came down with mononucleosis about a month before the state meet senior year. I was going after my 11th state title and was expected to win. My doctor told me I wouldn't be able to run for a few weeks. Of course I didn't listen, so, when I worked out, I told my parents I was going to the woods for a walk. Once I got around the corner, I would start running. I did this on a daily basis and when the time came, I insisted on running in the state meet. I won the race. Call it toughness or call it stupidity, it probably isn't a good example of what to do in a similar situation. I was lucky that time, but that hasn't always been the case. For example, in 1999, knowing my calf was extremely tight, I ignored the warning signs and ran an 800-meter event in an indoor meet in Boston. The results were spectacular. I set an American record in 1:58, but I tore my Achilles tendon in the process. The torn tendon definitely wasn't worth the record.

lesson #6: periodically take time

off Many runners, including myself, have experienced burnout. It's mostly a mental thing. When I first experienced burnout, I didn't know what it was. I just knew running was no longer fun. I had no confidence in my running and no motivation to train.

I went through this period shortly after my first Olympic Games back in 1992. I had experienced winning for years, but in Barcelona, I got my butt kicked. Losing was hard to swallow and difficult to get accustomed to. During this burnout period, individuals I had dominated in the past now beat me. The pressures of winning finally got to me and caused me to want to run away from the sport. How did I break out of this funk? It wasn't easy, and it took some time.

A new coach made it his goal to give the love of running back to me. The first thing he had me do was take a break. I didn't run for at least a month. I began to miss running quite quickly and realized it wasn't the running that caused my frustrations, it was the competing. I eased back into running, but knew competition would be a long way off. With no competitions on the horizon, I felt the pressure lift. As a few months passed, my goals were reduced. The object was not to be a world beater at this time. My only goal was to enjoy competition as I had in previous days.

I entered small time races locally, experiencing success in baby steps and slowly regaining confidence. By the time the U.S. Nationals rolled around in mid-1993, I was getting there. A fourth place finish there was good enough for me at that time. I knew people expected more from me, but I didn't care. It was a tough lesson to learn, but one that was essential. The confidence I was building allowed for better workouts and better racing. After about a year, I was ready to take on the world again.

time to erase those mistakes

Making mistakes is what helps us learn. But it's how you handle and learn from those mistakes that will determine your longevity in the sport. As you can see, I've made plenty of mistakes early in my career. I hear similar stories from peers and even have watched many go through the same things. I hope this book helps you and other female runners avoid some of those common mistakes that most young athletes make. In *Fast Track*, I have teamed up with Jose Antonio, Ph.D., to provide you with a complete guide to training, eating, and performing at the top of your game. *Fast Track* answers all the questions I had when I was younger, and I hope it will do the same for you.

Specifically, in part 1 I'll share some of my training secrets with you. In part 2, you'll learn how to avoid the common mistakes of young female runners. In part 3, we'll review some basic physiology, so you can better understand just how your body runs. In part 4, you'll learn how to fuel your running through proper nutrition. And, in part 5, you'll learn how to train for optimum success. I've tried to cover the major issues, issues that I found confusing at one point in my career, issues that became a lingering source of frustration for me for many years. Back then, I wish I had had a road map to follow, to avoid the many ups and downs I experienced. Now you have just that. Please use *Fast Track* as a resource to guide you down those tough roads and provide you with the answers you seek.

CHAPTER 2

Suzy's Turn-Around
how I became a consistent
sub-4:00-min 1500-meter runner

In my event, the 1500-meter run, you haven't really arrived on the scene until you have run under 4 minutes. I can remember back in the mid-90s thinking that a sub-4:00 was a pipe dream for me. My coaches and fellow runners told me I had the talent to go sub-4:00, but I didn't believe them. More important, I didn't believe in myself.

Until that point, my fastest time in the 1500 was a 4:04. Those last 5 seconds seemed like an impossible barrier to me. Yet, eventually, over time, with the right diet, training ingredients, and a can-do attitude, I was able to break the 4-minute barrier, over and over again. How did I become a 3:57 runner? Let me start from the beginning, in 1997, when I first began trying to break the 4-minute barrier.

From my college days to around late 1997, my running was at a bit of a standstill. At first, I blamed my lack of progress on my coaching. As a result, I switched coaches a couple of times during the early '90s.

Yet, the results were the same. I seemed stuck in this 4:04 1500-meter rut. I certainly wanted to run better, but at the time, I probably didn't want it enough. I was living a comfortable life and had plenty of opportunities off the track to keep me busy, in particular modeling, promotional appearances, and product endorsements. As a result, at that point in my life, running wasn't that important to me. I genuinely thought I was doing what I could to give myself the best chance for success on the track. Of course, looking back on those early days of my career, I now realize I wasn't fully committed to my training, and I certainly wasn't following the training or nutritional program that I needed to follow to go sub-4:00.

In the mid-90s, I was coached by Dick Brown in Eugene. He's a great coach and a wonderful man, but he used to drive me crazy with how much he sweated the details. He would always tell me, "Suzy, you have to do the little things if you want to be great." He was one of those people who thought I could be great, as good as Mary (Decker) Slaney was in her prime. He wanted me to eat right, take supplements, focus more on my mechanics, race less, and travel less. I rebelled against his advice. I didn't eat the best of foods. I didn't take my supplements. I didn't work on my mechanics. I traveled and raced even more. Of course, I humored him sometimes, but I also wanted to have a life. Although Dick and I didn't have the right chemistry to form the kind of relationship needed for greatness, I look back on those years and realize he was right about a lot of things. I just wasn't ready for his advice at that time in my career. I needed to get to a point in my life where I could see that.

Dick wasn't the only person I largely ignored. When people (and there were many) would suggest different training or dietary ideas, I would shrug them off. I was defensive, and would become a little upset when someone approached me and offered an opinion. I kept thinking, "Hey, I have to be doing something right to get to where I'm at, so why change?" I guess I was satisfied with my running and didn't want to make the changes or listen to new ideas. I guess I wasn't hungry enough for the sub-4:00 or for true racing success.

In 1997, things began to change. I had been a successful collegiate runner and a pretty good professional runner. My sponsors paid me well because of my collegiate record and had high expectations as a result. My sponsors wanted me not only to race well but also to have good marketability off the track. I hadn't lived up to expectations during the 1996 Olympics, and various people, particularly my sponsors, expected me to be great, not good.

I knew I could go only so far with my modeling off the track. When one sports writer labeled me the Anna Kournikova of track and field, it stung. I thought I had achieved a bit more than Kournikova, but I got the message. Around the same time, I was negotiating my contract with Nike, whose officials made it quite clear that they would not be willing to pay me the kind of money I had grown accustomed to for mediocre performance. They believed I could run faster than I thought I could, and threw incentives out there to boost my motivation. I decided it was time to make some changes.

I didn't figure it all out on one specific day. Yet, getting serious about my career was the first step in the right direction. I began to commit myself to my running, and I was willing to do the little things if need be, even if they were a pain in the butt. It has taken a long, long time to grow as a runner, and I'm still learning on an almost daily basis. What follows is a story about how I turned things around.

training smarter When Nike gave me that ulti-

matum back in late 1997, the first thing I did was move from Eugene, Oregon, back to Madison, Wisconsin, and back to my college coach, Peter Tegen. I quickly realized that Peter was going to train me differently than he had in college. The workouts would be roughly the same as back then, but the intensity would be increased dramatically, with a continued emphasis on speed. He taught me to work harder but smarter. I was training right on the edge and, from a philosophical perspective, differently from the way I had been training under my previous coach. The program, of course, was risky, making injuries more likely. Yet the rewards were greater.

We kept my weekly mileage the same. If anything, we decreased my miles a bit, placing a greater emphasis on quality workouts. Rarely did I run anything over 400 meters at practice. Instead, I did a ton of speed-work, sessions consisting of 200-meter, 150-meter, and 300-meter sprints. These fast-paced intervals usually included active rest. Rather than standing around and catching my breath, I jogged or did crunches or pushups. Every minute of practice counted. During each training week, I got more bang for every mile. Although I had lost some of my speed during the previous few years, it was amazing how quickly it came back. After 6 months of this new type of training, I was already outkicking those who had been blowing me away in the final stretch of the 1500.

In 1997 and 1998, my speed improved, and I was starting to see the results in faster racing times, including my first sub-4:00 1500-meter in Monaco in 1998. At the same time, it was becoming increasingly clear that I was running out of gas midway through the European circuit. For example, a week after the Monaco sub-4:00, I ran my next race in Zurich and finished 12th, 7 seconds slower than the previous week. I had no kick, little energy, and my practices were suddenly becoming difficult to complete. I was out of gas with a full month left in the season.

Why did this happen so suddenly? I had committed a fatal training error. I didn't concentrate on base training in the off-season. In fact, back then, I never really had an off-season to concentrate on. I would run a full outdoor season, get right into the road-racing season, then go straight to the indoor season, then back to the following outdoor season. Where was the time for base training? Fortunately for high school and collegiate runners, there's cross-country season, a great opportunity to build some quality base.

Most major meets, including the World Championships and Olympic Games, are at the tail end of the season. Peter and I knew we needed to add more strength to my arsenal if I was going to be able to consistently compete with the big girls. We shifted to a focus on base during the winter months, omitted indoor track and road racing, and concentrated solely on success during the outdoor track season. If there were any off-season races, they would be cross-country races or indoor races relying solely on base training.

We then moved away from speed just a bit, and focused more on strength(endurance). It was logical, considering that with my age, 31, my speed was going to slip a bit because of my achilles injury and my increasing age. In keeping with my newfound training-smart philosophy, the drive for better endurance would not be accomplished by an increase in mileage. Rather, I would incorporate longer intervals of 800 meters, 1000 meters, and even 3000 meters. I also added tempo runs into my weekly program.

These types of runs were completely foreign to me. The only time I had done something remotely similar was back in college during cross-country season. Why didn't we just increase the mileage? My body just couldn't withstand the miles it once could when I was younger. I knew I had to make the most of the miles I was able to run. I'm a believer that too many runners run junk miles—too many miles at low intensity. My personal opinion is that low-intensity runs are for recovery after a big event, not for getting fit.

The endurance training paid off. It made running at 1500-meter pace in a race feel easier. Hence, I felt stronger at the end of a race, with 200 to 300 meters to go, and could use my speed to its fullest during my kick. During the 2002 season, I was able to run the 1500 meters under 4 minutes three different times during a 3-week span. Amazingly, running that fast felt easy. It showed me what I can do when everything comes together. Proper strength training with a great base, proper speed training, appropriate rest, diet, and so on came together to help me achieve my goals. During that season, I finally realized that I had fulfilled my potential, that I was running the way I had always dreamed I'd run.

CHAPTER 3

Suzy's Sample Training and Eating Program
putting the pieces together

Over the years, I've learned that training is a lot like a jigsaw puzzle. If you don't put the pieces together properly, the puzzle just isn't going to work. Diet, cross-training, mileage, weight training, stretching, and massage are all parts of the bigger puzzle picture. They all have to work together if everything is going to fall into place.

In this chapter, I've outlined the pieces of my training puzzle that work together to make me a better runner. I've included how running mechanics, weight training, stretching, and supplements fill out the training picture. I've also included information about what I eat and why. For me, diet is the foundation for everything else. If you aren't fueled properly, your body will just run out of gas. Depending on your fitness level and your goals, you probably will not need to do the same workouts or even follow the exact eating plan that I do—that is, unless you, too, are training at the Olympic level. You'll learn everything you need to know to design the best training and eating plan for your fitness level and goals later in *Fast Track*. Use this chapter as a guideline to see how such puzzle pieces fit together to form a complete training picture.

beyond running
There's more to running well than, well, just running. Unfortunately, for me, I learned this lesson the hard way. I pretty much trained by running and only running until injuries started to become a factor. As a young runner back in the 1980s, I thought I was invincible. I thought I could eat anything I wanted and train any way I wanted. Working on my mechanics, lifting weights, stretching, and taking supplements? That stuff just wasn't important to me back then. As I began to age, however, I noticed that my body didn't handle food quite the same way. My body broke down more easily. My muscles felt tighter. Injuries popped up. Suddenly I paid attention to mechanics because my excessive "toe running" was causing too much strain on my body. I focused on lifting to keep my muscles strong so my tendons and ligaments wouldn't have to work as hard. I turned to stretching to prevent strains and pulls, and to my diet to stay lean. I began taking supplements for the health of my bones and blood. Here's how I now incorporate each into my overall training plan.

running form and mechanics

People have told me that I have great running form. Not so. Sure I run smoothly, but any expert on the subject of running form will tell you that my actual mechanics are not ideal. Although my mechanics have improved greatly over the past few years, I'm not as efficient as I could be. I still run way up on my toes, which can be quite strenuous on my Achilles (the likely cause of my Achilles tear back in 1999). I'm now making an active effort to run more flat-footed. Toe running is my form flaw. As I look around at young runners, I see that I'm not alone; almost every runner has flaws. Below, you'll find my coach Peter Tegen's five essential points on running mechanics.

1. Plant your feet at the mid-foot area or at a full-foot plant. Avoid a pure heel touchdown.
2. Angle your foot so that it's either pointing straight ahead at touchdown or pointing slightly inward, which is ideal. Avoid landing with your foot pointed out.
3. Run tall and upright. Don't "sit," lean forward, or lean back.
4. Swing your arms naturally, avoiding crossing them over your chest on the forward swing. Don't overuse your arm swing. Rather, keep your hands relaxed and loosely open.
5. Watch the horizon or a fence, building, or tree in front of you. This will keep your eyes looking forward and your head properly aligned, and prevent too much up and down motion.

weight training

I used to lift weights without a goal in mind. I'd simply do what I saw everyone else at the gym doing. As I've grown older, I've learned how important weight training is and how doing it properly can specifically help my running.

Basically, I lift 3 days a week (usually on the same days as my hard running workouts). I emphasize core strengthening and stretching, and also do quite a bit of bounding work (exaggerated knee lifts and strides). In the heart of the season, I decrease the intensity of my weight work-outs and concentrate more on recovery than big-time lifting.

I generally lift weights after a hard workout. A typical weight-training session includes the following:

- 15 minutes of stretching
- 25 minutes of my core routine, which consists of a series of 5 exercises, including 3 sets of 50 crunches, side-to-side sitting twists with a 6-pound medicine ball, and other exercises
- 3 sets of 12 single-legged squats (think *Karate Kid*)
- 2 sets of 25 pushups
- 2 sets of 10 to 12 pullups
- 2 sets of 12 single-leg hamstring curls
- 2 sets of 12 single-leg presses
- 2 sets of 12 single-leg extensions
- 2 sets of 12 multihip machine (forward and backward)
- 4 sets of 30 single-leg standing calf raises (just using body weight)
- 2 sets of 30 seated calf raises with 45-pound weights

cross-training

The body just isn't built for running every day without a break. If you don't give your running muscles a rest from time to time, your body will break down. Your mind can also become stale. For this reason, I'll occasionally take an entire day off. Sometimes I use cross-training as my entire daily workout, but more often I use it for a second workout in addition to my run. I cross-train 2 or 3 days a week, via the Nordic-track, the pool, or the stationary bike. Sometimes I cross-train at a steady moderate-to-easy pace; other times I go for a more serious, interval-based workout. It just depends on what my body needs at the time, how tired I am, and how my muscles feel.

Cross-training allows me to train without putting unnecessary stress on my body, so it helps me prevent injuries. On the rare occasions when I am injured, it helps me maintain my fitness. Most cross-training exercises strengthen the body and work different muscles than running does, which allows me to add extra volume to my training without beating up my body. Finally, cross-training provides a nice mental break.

Here is my favorite cross-training workout. In the pool, I run, completing an easy, 20-minute warmup. During the next 20 minutes, I alternate 1 minute very hard, the next easy, then repeat over and over. I finish up with a 20-minute cooldown.

stretching

Gerard Hartmann, my massage therapist, emphasizes the importance of stretching to prevent injuries. Besides the basic stretches most of us do, Gerard showed me how to increase my flexibility to a degree that I never thought possible. I'm more limber today than ever before, and hardly ever experience those little pulls and strains like I used to. The difference was in the intensity. I guess you could say that, until I met Gerard, I was a passive stretcher. I just went through the motions and didn't understand how far my muscles, tendons, and ligaments could be stretched. He introduced me to stretching with a rope and sometimes added his own body weight to mine to encourage me to go a bit farther, stretching me beyond the point I thought possible. The results were amazing. I felt great. Of course, he introduced me to new

Stretching has revolutionized my training.

stretches as well, targeting areas that had never really been worked. Simply put, I became an active stretcher because of Gerard's teachings.

my base season training plan

Peaking at precisely the right time has been an immense problem for me throughout my professional career. I certainly know the basics behind it, but circumstances have made it extremely difficult—and sometimes impossible—to do. So what mistakes have I made in this department? It all comes down to lack of base.

Base training for distance running is essentially building an endurance base first (aerobic base), just as you would build a good basement first when building a house. You can achieve this with longer, gentler, more even paced runs, keeping a comfortable running and breathing rhythm. As you get stronger, you might consider increasing the distance and eventually the pace as well. Base training is a long process of 2 to 3 months, so you'll need to be patient.

Without base, your peak is limited in its duration. During our outdoor season, we're expected to hold a peak for about 3 months. The National Championships take place in mid-June, and the season ends in mid-September. Without a great base, forget it. Year after year as a professional, I would start out my season in fine form, and then by August I'd fall apart, usually ending with a disastrous race, then prematurely calling it a season. So why was my base insufficient to get me through the entire season? Well, I used to really focus on the road-mile

The Dangers of Extending Your Peak

In the United States, our National Championships are always held at least 2 months before the major championship for the year, whether it be the World Championships or the Olympic Games. This requires one to peak for Nationals, and then either try to hold that peak for 2 months, or peak once for Nationals and then again 2 months later. In 2000, for example, Olympic Trials were held in mid-July. One week later, I ran 3:57 in Oslo, which made me one of the favorites in Sydney, but the Olympics were still 8 weeks away. By the time the Games arrived, I was a shell of my former self. I made it to the 1500 final, but collapsed with 100 to go. Here's the great news, however. Our federation has finally come to their senses, and in 2004 will hold the Olympic Trials only 1 month before the Olympics. I can't tell you what a welcome development that is. An extended peak won't be as necessary as in the past. All American track athletes should perform better at the Games as a result.

circuit, held in December and January, the indoor season, held in February and March, and even some of the early outdoor meets held in April. So where was the time for base training?

Starting in 1999, injuries began to pop up. I suffered a torn Achilles in 1999, then an avulsion fracture of my ischium (lower pelvis) in 2000. By this time I had decided to eliminate road miles and indoor races from my schedule, but it was the injuries that put me on the shelf during base time. So during the 2000 and 2001 seasons, I faded badly at the end of the season.

I finally learned how to peak at the right time by 2002. Why? I had a full base-training period during winter 2001 to 2002. Instead of competing during the indoor season, I ran cross-country, where the required training is similar to base training. I delayed speed work, and the start of my outdoor season as much as possible. The problem was I ran subpar in my early summer races as a result, but that was the sacrifice I had to make. I was able to run three sub-4:00s in August and September, including two over a 3-day period. I had finally proven to myself that a great base was the answer.

Below, you'll find how I now train during base season, to build my fitness for the season ahead.

Monday: 20-minute easy run, strides, 4 × 3 minutes on trails at a good clip. Light jog back in between. 15-minute cooldown. Weights.

Tuesday: 50-minute moderate run in afternoon with a few 30-second surges. In morning or evening, 20 to 30 minutes on stationary bike or Nordictrack, or aquarunning.

Wednesday: 20-minute easy run, strides, 6 × 300 on trails. Light jog back to start, then repeat. 15-minute cooldown. Weights (total body, just legs, or just arms).

Thursday: 50-minute moderate run in afternoon with a few 30-second surges. In morning or evening, 20 to 30 minutes on stationary bike or Nordictrack, or aquarunning.

Friday: 20-minute easy run, strides, then 15- to 20-minute tempo run with rocks in my hands (the small weight of the rocks does not alter your running mechanics, and yet, over a 20-minute period you get enough of a stimulus to develop some highly specific strength endurance). 15-minute cooldown. Weights.

Saturday: 1-hour recovery run (no surges). Cross-training (optional).

Sunday: Easy 30- to 35-minute run or day off, depending on how I feel.

racing season
During racing season, training is usually designed to sharpen and fine-tune the body. I'm trying to become speedier for those races that always seem to come down to the last 200 meters. My speed intervals become shorter, but I do more of them with shorter rest periods. I'm not overdoing the longer stuff, and I focus my workouts on quality as opposed to quantity. I don't want to overextend myself during this period because I want to be relatively fresh for races. I usually begin tapering 10 to 14 days before the goal meet (the World Championships or the Olympic Games). My workouts will get progressively shorter and the focus will be almost exclusively on quality. My coach likes to say at this point, "The hay is in the barn." I've done the hard work and now it's just time to let the body rest a bit and sharpen up for the big event.

Below you'll find what a typical week of workouts looks like during racing season.

Monday: 20-minute easy run, strides, diagonals, 4 × 300 meter progressions, 3 × 600 meters on track. 15-minute cooldown. Weights.

Tuesday: 45- to 50-minute moderate run with a few 30-second surges.

Wednesday: 20-minute easy run, strides, diagonals, 6 × 200 meter fast strides, 6 × 150 meters fast, fast strides. 15-minute cooldown. Weights.

Thursday: 30-minute easy run with a few strides.

Friday: Race or tempo run. Weights if no race.

Saturday: 1-hour recovery run (no surges).

Sunday: 30- to 35-minute run or day off, depending on how I feel.

how I changed my diet I met my coau-

thor, sports nutritionist, and exercise physiologist, Joey (Jose) Antonio, a couple of years ago. If it weren't for him, sometimes I think I may never have changed my diet and learned to eat right. As I mentioned before, my early diet consisted mainly of pasta, breads, pizza, and fast food. All I ever heard during my early professional career was "eat carbohydrates." Other runners always insisted that carbo-loading was the only way to go. So that's what I did. I ate tons of pasta and little else. I thought it was making me faster and stronger, but it was actually making me sluggish. Eating too many carbohydrates also made it difficult for me to become as lean as I wanted to be.

the four changes that improved my diet

With Joey's help, I made four major changes to my diet. They've worked for me so far. Hopefully, they'll work for you, too.

Eat low-glycemic foods. I used to have trouble keeping my energy levels up during my workouts and races. Even as recently as the 2001 World Championships, I had a bout of hypoglycemia (an abnormally low amount of sugar in the blood). It doesn't matter what shape I'm in: If low blood sugar hits me, then I run lousy. This was evident at Edmonton when I failed to finish the semi-finals. I'm pretty sure hypoglycemia was a factor in Sydney, too, when I blacked out with 100 meters to go in the Olympic final. By starting to eat low-glycemic/high-fiber foods (carbohydrates that break down slowly, releasing glucose gradually into the bloodstream), I found that I wasn't as worn out after practices and races. I now focus on veggies, apples, pears, whole-grain foods, oatmeal, and cheese.

Eat more protein. I used to have great difficulty getting my body as lean as I would like. Then I started emphasizing more protein in my diet (good options include eggs, lean meat, chicken, and fish). This helped keep my energy more constant during the day, without all the ups and downs. Proteins tend to digest slower than carbohydrates. The amount of protein I eat per day is proportional to my body weight (1 gram per pound of body weight, so 105 grams), though at times I eat even more than that. According to Joey Antonio, there's no harm in eating more protein. In fact, it may even be better (for muscle tissue repair).

Eat frequent, small meals throughout the day. A couple of years ago, after realizing that I was bonking (fatiguing early) way too much at workouts and in races, I started to eat smaller meals more frequently. I began eating protein bars and drinks as snacks before and immediately after workouts. I found that it kept my energy high and also helped speed up my metabolism. All around, it just made me feel better. It wasn't easy at first, but now I'm accustomed to it, and it has worked wonderfully for me.

Eat balanced meals. I eat tons of fish, chicken, and red meat, and usually have brown rice to go along with anything I eat. (White rice just provides empty carbohydrates, whereas brown rice provides important vitamins, minerals, and fiber.) The meals I eat are simple and routine, but they work for me.

translating the four eating strategies into daily life

I understand that it's one thing to know what foods to eat, but quite another to actually do it. The *Fast Track* eating plan in chapter 11 will provide you with a simple guide for incorporating these eating strategies into your life. For now, consider the following sample of my weekly diet just to get a better idea of how these eating strategies translate into true meals.

Monday

9:00 A.M. Half of a 35-gram protein shake, brown-rice cereal (maybe with a scoop of protein powder mixed in), yogurt, a couple strips of turkey bacon, and my daily supplements

11:00 A.M. The rest of my protein shake

1:00 P.M. Plain turkey sandwich with a Diet V8 Splash

3:00 to 6:00 P.M. I have practice, so I sip on a shake throughout the workout and finish the rest when practice is over. I also usually snack on a protein/energy bar during the practice. Also, I take 2,500 milligrams of glutamine just before practice.

6:30 P.M. Grilled swordfish with fruit salsa, brown rice, 2 chocolate chip cookies (I'm human), and mineral water

10:00 P.M. Slow-release protein shake

Tuesday

9:00 A.M. Half of a 35-gram protein shake, granola, rice cake with honey, yogurt, pineapple juice, and my daily supplements

11:00 A.M. The rest of my protein shake

Noon Run

1:30 P.M. Plain turkey sandwich with some mineral water

4:00 P.M. A protein/carbohydrate–balanced shake

6:00 P.M. Plain chicken sandwich, brown rice, sugar-free Jell-O with a little Cool Whip, and mineral water

10:00 P.M. A slow-release protein shake

Wednesday

9:00 A.M. Half of a 35-gram protein shake, muesli, rice cake with honey, yogurt, a couple strips of turkey bacon, grape juice, and my daily supplements

11:00 A.M. The rest of my protein shake

1:00 P.M. 1 chicken taco with salsa and a protein smoothie

3:00 to 6:00 P.M. I have practice, so I sip on a shake throughout the workout and finish the rest when practice is over. Also, I take 2500 milligrams of glutamine just before practice.

6:30 P.M. Grilled salmon with chipotle seasoning and fruit salsa, brown rice, and mineral water

10:00 P.M. A slow-release protein shake

Thursday

9:00 A.M. Half of a 35-gram protein shake, granola, rice cake with honey, yogurt, pineapple juice, and my daily supplements

11:00 A.M. The rest of my protein shake

Noon Run

1:30 P.M. Plain turkey sandwich and mineral water

4:00 P.M. A protein/carbohydrate–balanced shake

6:00 P.M. Grilled chicken on top of salad (no dressing), brown rice, sugar-free Jell-O, and mineral water

10:00 P.M. A slow-release protein shake

Friday

9:00 A.M. Half of a 35-gram protein shake, brown-rice cereal with protein powder, plain English muffin, yogurt, grape juice, and my daily supplements

11:00 A.M. The rest of my protein shake

1:00 P.M. 1 chicken taco with salsa and a protein smoothie

3:00 to 6:00 P.M. I have practice, so I sip on a shake throughout the workout and finish the rest when practice is over. Also, I take 2500 milligrams of glutamine just before practice.

6:30 P.M. This is my night to splurge. It's traditional to go out for Friday fish fry here in Wisconsin, so I'll have baked cod, rusti (hash browns with cheese), creamed spinach, and a glass of wine.

10:00 P.M. A slow-release protein shake

Saturday

10:00 A.M. Half of a 35-gram protein shake, granola, rice cake with honey, yogurt, grape juice, and my daily supplements

11:30 A.M. The rest of my shake

1:00 P.M. Run

2:30 P.M. Leftover baked fish from the night before

3:30 P.M. A protein/carbohydrate–balanced energy bar

6:00 P.M. ⅓ pound hamburger with only pickles

10:00 P.M. A slow-release protein shake

Sunday

10:00 A.M. Half of a 35-gram protein shake, muesli, yogurt, Diet V8 Splash, and my daily supplements

11:30 A.M. The rest of my shake and maybe some string cheese

1:00 P.M. Cross-train or day off

2:30 P.M. Plain turkey sandwich, a few soy-flavored rice chips, and mineral water

4:30 P.M. A protein/carbohydrate balanced energy bar

6:30 P.M. Soft chicken tacos with a little cheese and peppers, and mineral water

10:00 P.M. A slow-release protein shake

My Favorite Meals
The following meals not only are delicious but also provide the fuel I need to run my best.

- Pizza, thin crust, easy on the cheese, with sausage and mushrooms (maybe twice a month)
- Chicken casserole and broccoli
- Quiche (with broccoli, Swiss cheese, green peppers, mushrooms, and turkey bacon)
- Turkey burgers
- Stir-fry with steak or chicken

supplements and meal replacements

Three or four times a year, I get my blood analyzed to determine what nutrients are too low or too high in my diet. Depending on what my body is lacking, I then take specific supplements to bring my levels up to where they need to be. As I age, I find that this is becoming more and more important. Of course, as a runner, I need to be careful about which supplements I put in my body because I'm always subject to drug testing. I take only those supplements that are legal and will benefit my health and performance.

Because I'm constantly traveling or training, I don't always have access to easy meals. I used to compromise my diet by putting less-than-perfect things in my body, such as fast food. Not anymore. Now I carry protein shakes and bars with me just about everywhere I go. They are perfect meal replacements and great supplements when you need to balance out a meal with some protein. Today, there are even ready-to-drink protein shakes, so there's no need to mess with mixing powders.

My Favorite Snacks The following snacks work great in a pinch and help give a little energy boost.

- Rice cakes with honey
- String cheese
- Yogurt with granola
- Sugar-free Jell-O
- Grapes and apples
- Protein bars
- Muffins (My favorite muffin recipe includes carrots, apples, coconut, and protein powder.)

the benefits of massage There are

many types of massage, but I prefer deep-tissue therapy. I started getting regular deep-tissue therapy in the early nineties. I found that it
helped me recover from my workouts more quickly and aided in the
prevention and rehabilitation of minor injuries. I considered it a benefit at the time, but it soon became an essential part of my running life.

Back in 1999, I had Achilles surgery, and months later was still un-
able to run without pain. It was a very frustrating time for me, and I
thought my career might be over. I had tried everything but nothing
worked. I contacted Gerard Hartmann of Limerick, Ireland, because,
I was told, he was the best deep-tissue therapist around. Gerard agreed
to see me, and I was off to Ireland. Upon arrival at his clinic, I began

My Favorite Supplements Below you'll find
the supplements that I take regularly.

- Multivitamin/multimineral supplement—one a day for general health
- Vitamin C—1,000 milligrams a day to help with recovery and prevent colds
- Iron—15 milligrams a day to boost the oxygen-carrying capacity of my red blood cells and prevent anemia
- Calcium—1,000 milligrams a day to keep my bones strong and prevent osteoporosis
- Glutamine—5,000 milligrams a day to support my immune system and decrease perceived exertion during workouts
- Vitamin E—1,000 IUs for protecting muscle-cell membranes and maintaining a healthy heart
- Essential fatty acids—500 to 2,000 milligrams a day to help with blood flow and cardiovascular health
- Protein—at least 1 gram per pound of body weight per day for repairing muscle tissue

an extremely intense strengthening program along with the most painful deep-tissue treatments I had ever imagined. Therapy took place twice a day for 10 days along with all kinds of ultrasound, heat, and stimulation treatments. For the first 4 days, I had tears streaming down my face during each session, and I wondered at the time if competing was worth this much pain.

After those first few days, the pain subsided and I was back to running pain-free. It felt like a miracle. Since then, plenty of injuries have popped up, and Gerard has been there each time, turning a career-threatening injury into a thing of the past. People like Gerard don't grow on trees, but there are many competent therapists out there. Do some research, and find yourself a good one. Massage is simply an essential part of any good running program.

As far as how often to get massage, there is no specific number I can give you. It depends on the time of year. During the off-season, I'll see

---

Sleeping High, Training Low Because

I'm currently training in Wisconsin, I can't practice at altitude as I'd like to. However, an altitude tent is certainly the next best thing. Basically, it's a small tent that is placed over my bed, where a regulated amount of oxygen is pumped inside to simulate living at 9,000 feet. The science behind this invention is that living at altitude increases red blood cell count. So, the more red blood cells you have, the more oxygen you will have for working muscles, and the better you will perform. Runners have long been known to train at high altitudes to increase endurance. An altitude tent is certainly not cheap, a little burdensome, and a bit wacky, but if you're looking for a legal edge, this is it.

a therapist once a week, with my husband giving me some brief therapy before each of my runs. When I'm getting into racing season, I'll up the sessions to two or even three times a week. I prefer therapy just after my intense workouts or races. It helps to repair any damage that has taken place and flushes the lactic acid out of my legs. This allows me to be ready for the next workout or race. The night before a race, I prefer a light flush-out massage just for the relaxation and loosening effects.

You should know that deep-tissue therapy can be quite painful. Don't worry, unless you have an extreme situation it shouldn't bring you to tears as it has for me. It does, however, require some toughness. Try your best to relax. Communicate with your therapist when you feel especially sensitive areas. That will allow the therapist to get to the root of the problem.

CHAPTER 4

Suzy's Training Diary
a 3-month odyssey
through the 2003 season

As a runner, one of the smartest things you can do is keep a training diary. Keeping a daily record of your mileage, your workouts, your diet, your sore muscles, the weather, possible injuries, new shoes, the number of rest days you've taken, and so on can help you understand why things go right and why they go wrong. For example, if you're feeling sluggish one particular week, check your log to see what you've been eating. You might notice that you haven't incorporated enough meat or beans in your diet, which could be compromising your iron levels. Or perhaps your legs are feeling achy and your muscles are starting to twinge. Check your log to see the last time you bought new running shoes. If it's more than 500 miles ago, the reason for your aches and pains could simply be worn-out shoes. Just last year, I nursed a hamstring injury that I sustained right before the start of the outdoor season. By recording it in my training log, I will be able to look back on my notes to see how I dealt with it and what I can do to prevent a similar injury in the future.

For all the reasons mentioned above, I like to keep a training diary. The following are excerpts from my 2003 outdoor season. My training entries deal with how I felt leading up to the 2003 World Championships, the biggest meet of the year. I hope it'll give you an idea of how recording my daily training and diet helps keep me in balance.

Let me give you some background information so you can understand where I was with my training before the following entries. To this point, where I pick up in mid-May, 2003, I was in very good base shape. I had done little speedwork because there was no need for it at the time. Speedwork becomes important once the season begins, and at this point, the start of my season was 2 weeks away. I was training for two meets in particular: the U.S. Championships in mid-June and the World Championships in late August. At this stage in my training, I had just started to get into the more intense workouts. It's always a scary period because it's a big adjustment for your body and you're so susceptible to injuries. So here we go!

May 13, 2003

Went for a 65-minute run. Felt no pain for the first time since my hamstring injury. The therapy is really helping. We're doing a lot of negatives, only doing the lowering phase of hamstring curls. In the evening, I added a 20-minute aquarun.

May 14

Ran a full warmup. This consists of stretching, a 15-minute run, eight 100-meter strides, and diagonals. (For diagonals, I start at one corner of a soccer field and run hard to the opposite corner. I then jog behind the soccer goal to the other corner for my recovery, and then repeat another diagonal stride to the other corner of the field. I usually do 8 to 10 diagonals, total.) Then I did 2 × 200 at 30-second pace, 2 × 800 at 2:06, and then a final 800 meters at 2:13. These were my first 800s of the year. Very encouraging times this early in the season.

May 15

Day off.

May 16

Hard tempo run today for 15 minutes. Maintained a 4:50 pace or thereabouts. Felt good and recovered from the 800 repeat workout. Did weights and therapy afterward. (Weights consisted of lunges, single-leg press, leg extensions, multihip exercises, standing and seated calf raises, jumping exercises—where I jump back and forth and side to side over an object about a foot tall—hamstring curls, hip abduction and adduction, and plenty of core work.)

May 17

65-minute easy run.

May 18

40-minute aquarun.

May 19

Back to the track. Very pleased with this workout. Did full warmup, then did 4 × 200 with 200-meter jog in between. The 200s were 28, 29, 29, and 29. Did 4 × 400 with a 400-meter jog in between. The 400s were 60, 59, 59, and 61. Did 4 × 200 with a 200-meter jog in between, this time at race pace (33, 32, 31, 30). Finished with weights and therapy.

May 20

Massage day. 50-minute steady run. Felt a little sluggish today.

May 21

Easy track workout. (The Prefontaine Classic is only a few days away.) Full warmup; 2 × 300 at race pace (48–49); 2-minute jog, 7-minute rest, 2-minute jog; 4 × 250 progressions; then cooldown, weights, and therapy.

May 22

60-minute run.

May 23

Flew to Eugene. Arrived and did a 20-minute "shake out" run, then 6 × 100 strides. That's all. Race is tomorrow, so lots of sleep tonight. Chicken and rice for dinner.

May 24

My first race in about 9 months. Felt decent, but not quite in race shape. Pacesetter went out way faster than she was supposed to, so we just let her go. I had to do all the work the entire race up front. An 800-meter gal from Slovenia outkicked me at the end. She ran a big PR and didn't show any appreciation for me towing her along. The kind of thing I'll remember. No big deal, it's early. Most important, I came out of the race healthy, not an easy thing to do after my first race.

May 25

Aquarun for 70 minutes. Good to be in the water today after the pounding of the track yesterday.

May 27

Full warmup. 4 × 200 with 200 jog in between at 29, 28, 29, 28. Then 5-minute rest, then 4 × 400 with 400 jog in between at 59, 60, 61, 61. Then 5-minute rest, then 4 × 200 with 200 jog in between at 30, 29, 30, 29. Jog down. Weights and massage.

May 28

50-minute recovery run. Felt pretty good. We're training through this next race on Saturday, so tomorrow's workout will be a challenge.

May 29

Full warmup, then 4 × 300 at 45, 45, 45, 44. Jog in between the 300s. 5-minute rest, then 3 × 700, focusing on the last 300: 400 at 67, 300 at 45; 400 at 63, 300 at 46; and 400 at 64, 300 at 46. 15-minute cooldown. Weights and massage.

May 30

50-minute recovery run.

May 31

Day before the race. Travel to Long Beach. Typical prerace workout.

June 1

Race in Los Angeles. Rabbit went out in 64, then 66. She did a much better job than the gal in Eugene. It still felt a bit slow, and my stride felt choppy. I finished 2nd to Regina Jacobs. She ran terrible in Mexico City and looked average in Eugene, but she looked very good today. I don't know how she does that. She complained about the pace being too slow. Perhaps if it's too slow for her, she ought to push the pace instead of letting me do it every race. Can't have your cake and eat it too! I ran another 4:03, so I can't be too upset about that, considering we were training through this race. I know I'll benefit down the road from all the work. Next race is Nationals in 3 weeks.

June 2

Felt surprisingly good today. 60-minute steady run. Therapy and weights.

June 3

Tough workout today. Full warmup, then 5 × 100 at 14.2, 14.3, 14.4, 14.5, 14.0 with 300-meter jog in between. Rest 2-5-3, then 4 × 200 at 27.4, 28.0, 28.9, 28.9 with 200-meter jog in between. Rest 2-6-4, then 3 × 300 at 43, 45, 45 with 300-meter jog in between. Had a massage.

June 4

50-minute recovery run, weights, and therapy.

June 5

20-minute aquarun, then later in the day, full warmup ten 6 × 150 with a walk-back, then 8 × 200 at 32 pace with a 100 jog and 100 walk-back. 15-minute cooldown.

June 6

45-minute recovery run.

June 7

Felt very tired today when I woke up. Full warmup, then 2 × 250 progressions, then 3 × 800 (200 at 29–30, 400 at 64–65, 200 at 30–31). I did the 800s in 2:06 (tough), 2:07 (felt better), 2:06 (best one). 15-minute cooldown. 20-minute aquarun later tonight.

June 8

60-minute recovery run.

June 9

Felt great today. Best track workout yet this year. Full warmup. 4 × 100 at 14.0, 14.2, 14.3, 13.7, with 100 jog in between. 5-minute rest. 3 × 200 at 28.0, 29.0, 28.2, with 200 jog in between. 5-minute rest. 2 × 300 at 42.5, 44.2, with 300 jog in between. 5-minute rest. 2 × 400 at 58.8, 61.9, with 400 jog in between. 15-minute cooldown, then 20-minute pool workout later.

June 10

Felt pretty good, a little sluggish. 50-minute recovery run, lifting, and therapy.

June 11

Full warmup, then a 15-minute tempo. Felt okay. Then did 5 × 250 progressions. Tweaked my butt muscle. It was tight from lifting the other night.

June 12

45-minute recovery run.

June 13

Time trial of 1000 meters today. Practicing going out hard so I can be ready for European racing. Mark (my husband) said I looked incredible today. First I did 2 × 200 at 30 and 31, and then I ran the 1000. First 200 designed to go out very fast, then take it down a notch for the next 600, then finish with a 200 kick. Did first 200 in 30, then 600 at 1:36, then the final 200 in 29. Ran a total of 2:36 in flats on a windy day, so I'm ecstatic.

June 14

60-minute recovery run. Little sluggish today.

June 15

Day off.

June 16

Full warmup, then 6 × 120 with walk-back for rest, then 2-6-3 for rest, then 6 × 200 with walk-back for rest. Weights and therapy.

June 17

45-minute steady run. Felt good.

June 18

Leave for Nationals today. Usual warmup and "shake out" strides.

June 19

Morning jog for 15 minutes, then heats of the 1500 tonight. I was in the second heat. A gal named Tiffany McWilliams was in my heat. She had just won NCAAs in 4:06, and I was told she always goes out really fast for the first lap, but then slows way down. I'm hoping in the final she will go out fast so she can tug me along for a lap. The faster we go out, the better for me. I won my heat in 4:11 or so, and McWilliams did go out fast, but I didn't follow her tonight. No need. I passed her at the end of the race and I think she was 2nd.

June 20

Easy day. Ran 15 minutes and 4 × 100 strides. Lots of protein for dinner. Salmon and rice.

June 21

We debated two strategies today. We know it's to my advantage to go out fast. My American rival, Regina Jacobs, is the better kicker, even though she's almost 40, but in a really fast race, her kick isn't as effective. That's why I beat her at races in Europe, where the races always go out fast. I wanted to go out with McWilliams for the first 400, then pass her, and push the pace hard. My coach, Peter, wanted me to wait until 600. My coach won. I would argue I was right because waiting allowed the pace to slow considerably after 400 meters. McWilliams always slows way down after the first 400. That slowdown allowed Jacobs to rest a bit after the fast start, and she had plenty of kick in the last 300 meters of the race. I need a faster pace to beat Jacobs at this time of the year. I have to be in 100 percent shape to beat her in a moderately paced race, and I'm *nowhere near 100 percent now. Jacobs's kick was especially good today, (Jacobs tested positive for a designer steroid, THG, at this meet, so that may explain the kick), but things will be different in a month or so.*

June 22

65-minute recovery run. Felt surprisingly well.

June 23

Full warmup, then 3 × 800 with last 300 being fast. Went out in about 65 on these and finished the last 300 in around 44. Rest in between was 2-5-3.

June 24

55-minute recovery run. Weights with emphasis on core today.

June 25

Full warmup, then 6 × 150 very fast. Then alternate 400s and 200s. 400s designed to go around 62–63, 200s around 31. After each 400, walk 100, then go into the 200, then walk 100. Today I was tired when I first started running, but I felt pretty good once I got going.

June 26

50-minute steady run with weights, then massage and therapy.

June 27

15-minute tempo run after full warmup. Fastest tempo run of the year. I always run my tempos on the same trail, so it's easy for me to mark my progress throughout the year. Felt very strong. I fly to Amsterdam this evening.

June 28

Arrived in Amsterdam early in the morning. Slept a few hours on the plane. I usually stay in a town called Nijmegen where my manager has a base set up. *Many of his athletes stay here. Mostly Kenyans and Ethiopians. There are great trails and a track within a quarter-mile, so it's perfect. Just after I arrived, I ran 35 minutes and felt pretty good. Then I took a 2-hour nap, had dinner, and went to sleep at 9 P.M. I was out in a minute.*

June 29

Today was a 55-minute run with some pickups. I felt a little bit off today. Jet lag! Took a nap and felt a little better. Still have a little dizzy feeling.

June 30

Woke up today not feeling great. I have a cold, no doubt. I'm scheduled to compete in Paris in a few days, but that looks in doubt. Rome is the next week, so I'll probably be shooting for that. Maybe the cold will pass quickly. So vulnerable to these type of things when you travel. Still did a workout today. 6 × 100 strides and 3 × 800. The 800s were not terribly quick because of how I was feeling, but I tried to emphasize the last 200, and those went well. Rested 2-5-3 in between.

July 1

50-minute recovery run.

July 2

20-minute morning run on the trails. Afternoon track workout. 4 × 300 in 45–46 range. First 100 at mile pace, second at 800 pace, last at fast stride. 2-8-2 for rest. 6 × 180 focusing on last 100. Last 100s were 13.2–13.7. 2-6-2 for rest. 600 at 32, 32, 30. 2-4-3 for rest. 500 at 31, 30, 14.0. Light weights and a flush out massage. My Achilles was a bit sore after the workout. I decided not to run in Paris because of the little bug I came down with and the Achilles acting up a bit. Feeling much better, but no need to chance it with big races coming up.

July 3

40-minute run in the woods. Calves were tight from yesterday's workout, so I took it easy. No pain in the Achilles today after treatment.

July 4

Speed workout on track. We weren't sure about this workout because of my calf tightness. Warmup went well, so we decided to go ahead. Strong wind today. 5 × 100, jog 300 in between. 13, 13, 13, 14, 14. 2-5-3 for rest. 4 × 200, jog 200 in between. 28, 30, 29, 29. 2-5-3 for rest. 3 × 300, jog 300 in between. 44, 45, 45. 2-6-2 for rest. 2 × 400, jog 400 in between. 60, 62. 12-minute cooldown. Happy with the workout. Felt strong, but the wind made it difficult. Massage. Calf feels better.

July 5

65-minute run in the woods. Felt slow for first 5 minutes, then got warmed up and actually felt pretty good. Core work and weights.

July 6

Took the day off.

July 7

20-minute morning run. Evening track workout. 4 × 300 at 43, 45, 44, 43. Jog 300 in between. 2-5-2 for rest. 6 × 130, focusing on the last 100s. 12, 12, 13, 13, 13, 13. 2-5-2 for rest. 600 at 32, 30, 29. 2-4-2 for rest. 500 with last 100 at 13.5. 20-minute cooldown. Felt really strong in my finish of the 600 and 500. Faster than last week.

July 8

I'm thinking about running Madrid the week after Rome because I missed the race in Paris. Ran 50 minutes easy. Felt good after 15 minutes or so. Light weights and massage. No pain in Achilles. Felt it once tonight when

I got up from the couch. I think calf raises tighten up my calves, and that causes my Achilles to be a bit tight on my first step.

July 9

40-minute, easy morning run with four 30-second surges. Surges felt very easy. Flew to Rome in the evening. Arrived late. Meet hotel has been moved closer to the city and the stadium, so that's good, but it's a bit noisy. I always bring earplugs to meets.

July 10

Bed was bad, so I have a bit of a stiff back. Massage tonight should help that. Protein shakes arrived this morning from the United States. My diet has been slacking a bit without those. I rely on them so much. Easy run with a few strides.

July 11

This morning we missed breakfast, but that's normal because I sleep until 10 or 11 during race season. No hurry to get up because I don't race until late tonight. It's hot here, but it will be better in the evening. Noon: "shake out" run. About 12 minutes. Not much to do. Just sit around the hotel, rest, and have lunch and an early dinner (I like chicken 3 hours before races; slow digesting, so I have long lasting energy). The race: Warmup went well. I just do a 15-minute easy run and a few strides. To the call room 20 minutes before the race, then out to the track for a few last-minute strides. Race was behind schedule so we sat around a bit and waited. So many people in this race. About 23, I think. Crazy. Very rough at the start, so I made my way up front. My manager had the pacesetters go 1100 meters. That was great. Usually I can only expect 800 meters of help. Went through 400 at 1:02, 800 at 2:07, 1200 at 3:12, and I finished 3rd in 4:01. Got passed on the final straight. Felt a little underraced. These gals have been racing, and it showed. The pace felt like a bit of a shock to me. I needed that. It will help for my next one, and those down the road. I kept clipping the heels of the Russian woman in front of me. She likes to push the pace, so it's always nice to race her. She was ranked #2 in the world in 2001, but was 17th tonight. The Olympic champ was also in the race and finished 18th. All in all, I felt okay.

1st	*Olga Yegorova*	*4:01.00*
2nd	*Natalia Rodriguez*	*4:01.30*
3rd	*Me*	*4:01.69*
4th	*Kelly Holmes*	*4:01.96*
5th	*Jo Pavey*	*4:02.03*

Had really good massage and a big dinner. Probably a bit too much pasta—but hey, it's Italy! Painful cross-friction on my Achilles. The massage is getting me through the training and racing, but it's a bit of a concern.

July 12

Flew back to Amsterdam. Had the day off. Long day of travel.

July 13

65-minute recovery run. Felt pretty well, all things considered.

July 14

20-minute morning run. We've trained through every race this season (focusing on Worlds at end of Aug), and this will be nothing different. Even though there is a race this weekend, I did a very challenging workout today. We did it on the trails instead of the track to ease the strain on my Achilles and calves. Did 2 × 800 on the trail. First in 2:06. Only 2-4-2 recovery. Then second in 2:05. 15-minute cooldown. Core exercises and light weights. Very happy with how this went. We've been focusing on minimal rest all season and I'm starting to see the benefits. In years past, I've taken at least 10-minute rest in between 800s, and never run them faster. I might pay for this in the race on Saturday, but I know it's going to help long term.

July 15

50-minute run in the forest. Light flush out. Found out today I'm ranked #1 in the World by IAAF. Wow!

July 16

20-minute morning run. Evening track workout: 4 × 300 at 44 seconds. 4 × 200 at 29, 28, 27, 27. Felt really strong today. I noticed it when I was warming up.

July 17

Travel to Madrid. 40-minute park run with a few surges. Little sluggish. Didn't sleep too well last night. Told to ice my Achilles 3 times a day. Seems to be helping.

July 18

Just hung out at the hotel. Very hot outside. Ran 15 minutes around the hotel and did a few strides around 8:00 P.M., the time of the race tomorrow. Difficult because the hotel is in the city center. Achilles feels better today from just 2 days ago. Don't feel sluggish tonight.

July 19

Slept till 11:00. Missed breakfast again. I am armed with my protein shakes now, so no big deal. Today will be another slow day at the hotel. If anybody thinks this job is glamorous, I wish they could see me now. There is so much downtime right now, it's embarrassing. Picked up my racing number after lunch. Field is big again (21), and quite good. This meet now has super-grand-prix status, which means more money, so the field is better than in years past. Took a 40-minute nap today, ate, and then left 2 hours later on the bus for the race. The buses always have police escorts, so I'm never worried about being late. Warmup track was inside, so it was cool. My race was at 9:10, so heat wasn't really a factor anyway. The race had lots of pushing at first again with so many people trying to get out front. I just hung back and let them do their thing. Plenty of time to catch up. The rabbit took off and I noticed nobody wanted to go with her, so at 250, I came up on the pacesetter. Pace felt more comfortable than last week. We go through the first lap in 65, a second off the 64 target pace I asked for, but that's okay, and not the rabbit's fault. She held back waiting for someone to catch up to her. She's a Russian gal, who's a very good 1500-meter runner in her own right. Just going for the win, so time isn't a big deal. We go through 800 in 2:09. Feeling better than last week. Just a bit sluggish with 400 to go, so instead of taking off, I decide to wait for someone to come up on me. Jo Pavey comes up on my side down the backstretch, so that's when I take off and win in 4:02. Everyone seemed a little tired for this race. Two runners didn't finish. I had a chance to watch the women's 3000 after my race. It's rare that I get a chance to actually watch a meet, so it was nice to sit down and watch the last race of the night. Had deep massage on my calves and Achilles. Very painful treatment, but the injury survived the race fairly well. I felt it a little when I did a few strides in my spikes before the race, but that was it. I talked to my coach, Peter, after the race. Very tough training for the next 3 weeks until Zurich. We've been saving my favorite workouts for the right time. Had a hard time falling asleep. Always the case after a good race.

July 20

Day off. Long day of travel (our train in Holland was delayed several hours because of an accident). Ice and massage.

July 21

65-minute long run. Felt good today. Could have raced if I had to.
Massage and ice. Weights and core.

July 22

50-minute run with 6 × 100 surges. Tomorrow we step up the workouts
in the final push toward Worlds.

July 23

Warmup, then 20-minute run on a straight, flat trail. 1 minute very hard,
the next more moderate, then continue to alternate. You try to keep the
off minutes pretty fast, but it's difficult to do after about 10 minutes.
Very tough mentally to do this, but it went well. 15-minute cooldown.
Ice and massage.

July 24

55-minute trail run.

July 25

20-minute morning "shake out" run. Afternoon trail workout. Full
warmup. 3 × 1 mile. First in 4:34, second in 4:31, third in 4:32. Hardest
workout so far this year, but I love this workout. First mile I felt a little
tight. Maybe not quite warmed up. Went out too fast. Second mile felt the
best. Felt more in control of pace. Third was mentally tough. Cooldown,
weights, and core. Massage and ice. Best I've felt physically in a while.

July 26

60-minute recovery run. Felt recovered. Could have raced today. Calves
a little tight.

July 27

20-minute morning run. In evening, full warmup, then another trail
workout. Trying to stay away from track to ease tension on calves and

Achilles. 3 × 800 first 2 slightly uphill. Both in 2:07. 6-minute rest in between. Last 800 slightly downhill run in 2:00. After each 800, I rested 20 seconds, then did a 30-second sprint. Cooldown. Trying to go out in these 800s very fast. Worlds final will go out very fast. Massage, ice, weights, and core.

July 28

Day off. Lactic acid in the legs a bit today. Flush out massage felt good.

July 29

60-minute trail run. Felt great, very strong. 6 minutes faster than usual.

July 30

Trail workout. Speed day. 4 × 200 in 29, 29, 28, 28 with walk-back rest. 2-6-2. 4 × 400 in 59, 59, 58, 58 with walk-back rest. Happy with these considering they're on the trails. 2-8-4. 2-mile tempo. First mile in 4:39, second in 4:54. Felt really good. 15-minute cooldown. Weights and core.

July 31

55-minute recovery run. Bit tired today. Didn't feel like sprinting. No surges.

Aug 1

Warmup and strides. 6 × 200. All in 28 except the last in 27. 2-6-2 for rest. 20-minute run again 1 minute hard, 1 easier. Went better than last week's same workout. Felt more used to it. Fast 400s were run around 61–62. Cooldown, strength, and core. Therapy and ice.

Aug 2

55-minute evening run. Felt pretty good, but took it easy for tomorrow's workout. This will be my sixth really hard workout. Another week of this, and then I begin my taper.

Aug 3

Trail run. Was going to run 3 × 1 mile today, but was feeling around 90 percent so I did the regular warmup, then 2 × 400 in 60 seconds. 2-6-2 for rest. Then 1 mile on the trail. Ran it in 4:26. Very pleased. Felt very strong the last 200. 2-7-2 for rest, then 5 × 300 progressions. Felt strong. Cooldown, therapy, and ice.

Aug 4

Day off. Museum day in Amsterdam.

Aug 5

50-minute trail run. Therapy and ice.

Aug 6

50-minute trail run. Weights and massage. Had cross-friction on my Achilles. It was painful but it felt better afterward. I need my body to hold up because I'm in the best shape of my life. I want to get out and race and put all this hard work into a great run.

Aug 7

Full warmup. First 5 minutes Achilles was sore. 2 × 400 in 60. 2-4-2 for rest. 3 × 1000, with rest being 2-4-2. First was 2:40, second was 2:41, third 2:40. Cooldown then treatment.

Aug 8

My birthday. My Achilles has been bothering me a little more the past few days than before, so we decided to give it a rest from running, so I did an aquarun. 70-minute aquarun with 6 × 1-minute intervals. I was a bit upset today because of my Achilles. Sometimes we don't have control over these things, so I can't panic. I just need to do everything I can to make the situation the best it can be. My emotions were up and down all day and I don't like that at all. I felt so much better after aquarunning. It was an instant feeling of goodness. Exercise will do that for me.

Aug 9

1 hour of aquarunning with 10 × 1-minute intervals.

Aug 10

My therapist, Gerard, suggested I try running. Achilles not feeling good at all. Call it a day after warmup. I'm very upset!

Aug 11

1 hour of aquarunning. Intervals. Going to Ireland for treatment. I hope Gerard can help.

Aug 12

Tried to jog and every step hurt. I'm worried about Worlds. No way will Zurich be happening for me.

Aug 13

Flew to Ireland. Biked for an hour. Felt easy. Did 6 × 3-minute with 3-minute rest.

Aug 14

Two treatments. Cross-friction very painful. Biked 1 hour. 6 × 2 minute with 2-minute rest. 6 × 1 minute with 1-minute rest. Felt good.

Aug 15

Cross-friction felt better. Biked 50 minutes with a few pick-ups. A little tired and emotionally drained today.

Aug 16

Biked 55 minutes. Did 1 minute hard, 1 minute easier for 20 minutes. Hard workout. Felt good.

Aug 17

Two more treatments. Gerard says we will make decision on Worlds in a couple of days. I'm improving, but he's worried that the tendon is vulnerable, and he's seen too many athletes in this position try to race and rupture their tendon. He keeps saying next year is so much more important being an Olympic year. More bike work. Haven't lost any fitness.

Aug 18

Was able to run relatively pain-free today. Much better, but certainly not perfect yet.

Aug 22

Decision made to call it a season. Not worth the risk.

It's amazing how fast a minor injury can turn into a major one. The same thing happened to me in 2002, and I was able to baby my way through it, but not this time. We probably got a little too greedy with the workouts because they were going so well. You always want a little more. After the therapy and the rest, my Achilles and calf were about 90 percent, which required one more trip over to Ireland to break up a little dead tissue. My Achilles will always be an issue, but as long as I'm on top of it (I plan on making prescheduled trips to Ireland every 2 months now), I should be fine. Anyway, from my last entry, I took my customary 3 weeks off, and then eased back into running, starting with 25-minute runs, and progressing roughly 5 minutes each week until I reached hour runs. That is the usual return-to-running plan, regardless of whether or not there is an injury. Getting back into things too rapidly almost always leads to little problems.

PART 2

Learning from Your Mistakes

CHAPTER 5

How to Run and Eat
top ten dos and don'ts
for young female runners

In part 1 of this book, Suzy revealed the mistakes she has made as a runner, and how they hindered her career. She also told you how she turned things around and became a consistent sub-4:00-min 1500-meter runner. As Suzy's experience shows, no amount of genetics or innate talent can overcome a poor diet or training plan. All of us, from the genetically gifted Olympian to the recreational runner, can go farther and faster if we focus on the right training ingredients and ignore the wrong ones.

That's, of course, easier said than done. One of the biggest challenges is knowing which ingredients to put in your training recipe and which ones to leave out. Misinformation abounds. Throughout this book, we'll give you precisely the information you need to know to create the perfect training recipe for your body. We'll dispel the myths, giving you the latest science on nutrition, supplements, and workouts. It all starts with the following training dos and don'ts.

do . . . educate yourself
When it comes to finding the best training and eating plan for you, your first step is knowing who to trust for information. Too often, runners turn to other runners for advice. This can backfire. If your roommate, best friend, and fellow runner tells you that jelly beans are a health food, don't go out and buy a bagful and eat 'em as you watch reruns of *Real World*. Also, don't believe your fellow runner when she says that eating one meal a day is the key to her running success. Even if it works for her, it may not work for you. In fact, it would probably be disastrous.

So, don't believe everything your friends tell you. Your most trustworthy sources of information include your cross-country coaches, track coaches, and conditioning coaches. These people have studied running, exercise physiology, and nutrition. They've seen firsthand how various training methods work or don't work. That's why they are your coaches—they know more about training than you! We implore you to listen to your coaches. As for fellow runners, it's probably safe to trust the advice of those who have been around long enough to remember who the president of the United States was *before* Ronald Reagan. Runners who are successful into their late 20s and 30s know more about running than an 18-year-old out of high school. Surround yourself with people who have more experience and know more about running than you. That's the key to long-term success.

do . . . eat dairy and meat
Many runners pile starchy carbohydrates onto their plates. The more bananas, potatoes, pasta, or bagels the better, they reason. Yes, it's true

that your running body needs carbohydrates for energy, but it also needs lean sources of protein. When you overdo it on the carbs, you'll compensate by underdoing it on the protein.

You need protein to help your muscles recover from a killer workout on the track or a long endurance run. After a workout, you have small tears in your muscle fibers. To repair this damage, it's essential that you eat plenty of protein. Most sources of protein contain important nutrients, such as calcium, iron, and zinc, which your running body needs. You need calcium for bone health and for fat burning, iron for red blood cell formation, and zinc for immunity. Many runners, however, are deficient in these nutrients, typically because they skimp on the foods that provide the nutrients.

If you thought milk was only good for dunking chocolate chip cookies, think again. Milk is an excellent source of protein and calcium. It contains many "bioactive peptides," little proteins that help improve your overall health. These peptides have been shown in numerous scientific reports to support the immune system and improve overall health. Milk also provides all of the amino acids that your running body needs. Also, did you know that the calcium in milk might help you burn more fat? In a new study released from the University of Tennessee, researchers stated, "Increasing dietary calcium results in significant reductions in adipose tissue mass in obese humans in the absence of caloric restriction and markedly accelerates the weight and body fat loss secondary to caloric restriction, whereas dairy products exert significantly greater effects. These data indicate an important role for dairy products in both the prevention and treatment of obesity." What that means in plain English is this: The more calcium you consume, the more fat your body burns, even if you aren't cutting back on calories.

Besides drinking more low-fat or fat-free milk, you should also consume one or two servings of beef per week (unless you're a vegetarian). Beef is a great source of protein, zinc, and iron. Unfortunately, many types of beef also come laden with artery-clogging saturated fat, which is one reason why you may be avoiding eating it. You can still have your beef and cut back on saturated fat by choosing leaner cuts, such as sirloin. (See "The Right Cut.")

do . . . eat fat
Despite what you may have heard, not all types of fat are bad for you. Many female runners make the huge mistake of trying to eliminate fat from their diet to lose weight. Yet you need to eat some fat daily for optimal performance. In fact, certain beneficial fats may prolong your endurance and boost your immunity. On the other hand, some types of fats are bad for your health. Continue to cut back on the bad fats: saturated fats and trans fats. Saturated fats are

---

The Right Cut
Consult this chart when purchasing beef at the grocery store.

FAT CONTENT OF DIFFERENT TYPES OF BEEF

	LEAN	FAT
Ground beef	70%	30%
Ground chuck	80%	20%
Ground round	85%	15%
Ground sirloin	90%	10%

Note: Figures are rounded.

---

found mainly in meats and other animal products. Chose low-fat or fat-free options, such as low-fat cheeses and milk and leaner cuts of meat, to cut back on this fat. Trans fats (listed on food labels as "partially hydrogenated" oils) may be worse for you than saturated fat. Trans fats increase levels of the "bad," or LDL, cholesterol in your blood. Most processed foods, including crackers and commercially baked goods, contain some trans fats, so read labels and avoid foods that list partially hydrogenated oils among the first few ingredients.

Then there are good fats! These are the unsaturated varieties. Both polyunsaturated and monounsaturated fats are healthy. Olive oil, fish, fats from nuts (such as cashews, macadamia nuts, and almonds), and avocados are healthy. Try to get at least a quarter-cup serving of healthy fats from nuts or olive oil every day. You need these fats to maintain the integrity, or health, of your cell membranes. This is especially important in promoting recovery from a hard workout or race.

do . . . eat immediately after training or racing Scientists have discovered that

if you eat a small meal immediately after training, you'll recover much more quickly than if you wait 2 hours. Just after a workout or race, your muscles will most quickly absorb the carbohydrate calories that you feed them. They will also take the protein you eat and put it to good use, rebuilding muscle fibers and repairing tissues. If you miss this important 2-hour window, the repair and recovery process takes much longer and you may feel sluggish in your subsequent workouts as a result.

If you want to recover faster and feel better the next day, you need to consume 250 calories of a combination of carbohydrates *and* protein right after training. The amount of carbs should be roughly twice as much as the protein. For example, if you're a 120-pound runner, we'd suggest you get roughly 20 grams of protein, 40 grams of carbohydrate, and a touch of fat (such as 1 teaspoon of flax oil).

Some athletes prefer a tad more protein because they feel it further expedites their recovery process. What's important is that you consume carbs and protein within 2 hours after training. The exact ratio of carbs to protein isn't as critical. This doesn't mean you should eat a peanut butter and jelly sandwich, because the protein in peanuts is inferior to animal sources. Instead, we recommend you consume a protein shake right after training. This will provide the nutrients your muscles crave right after intense exercise.

don't . . . eat like a pow (prisoner of war)

Undereating is probably the most common mistake that female runners make. How can you possibly feel normal when you're running 40 miles a week but eating fewer calories than your pet hamster? Granted, a hamster can run on that exercise wheel for hours on a diet of seeds and hamster chow—but you aren't a hamster. You need calories! It's true that thinner, leaner runners tend to be the fastest runners. That doesn't necessarily mean you'll run better at 12 percent body fat versus 15 percent body fat. Each runner has a different build; some are naturally lean, and others have naturally wider hips and thicker bones. Don't kill yourself trying to attain the body of some other runner. Work with the stuff your mom and dad provided (that is, your genetics). You'll go farther and faster by putting fuel in your tank than you will by starving yourself to lose weight. So eat, please.

don't . . . treat bagels as a
health food Bagels and pretzels are popular among runners because they are low in fat. Yet they are among the worst foods you can possibly eat. Eating a bagel is no more nutritious than opening a packet of table sugar and pouring it down your throat. Like table sugar, bagels rank high on the glycemic index (GI), a measure of how quickly a food breaks down and spikes your blood sugar. Foods that break down too fast raise your blood sugar level too high too fast, causing it to crash a short while later. Not long after eating a bagel or some other type of empty carbohydrate, you will feel tired and hungry all over again.

Bagels simply have few redeeming qualities. They contain little fiber and no protein or other nutrients. Just for comparison, let's look at a plain bagel with 2 tablespoons of jam versus a McDonald's Quarter Pounder sandwich (see "Surprising but True" on page 68). Of course, a Quarter Pounder does not qualify as a "health food," but it actually provides a more balanced meal than a bagel with jam. The bottom line is this: Don't eat a food, especially a high-carbohydrate food, simply because it's low in fat. It may be low in nutrients as well. With the exception of immediately after a workout, limit your intake of high-GI items like bagels, white bread, and white pasta. Also, if you're doing a long run lasting more than 90 minutes, it might help to consume a high-GI carb during the run. There are various gel packs that could meet this need.

don't . . . train for the western states 100-mile race when you'll be racing the 1-mile race

Imagine this. You start running from Squaw Valley, California, and end up in Auburn, California, 100 miles later. That's the Western States 100-mile race. The winner of the 2003 race finished in 16:01:18 (that's more than 16 hours). His average pace was 9:37. The poor soul who

---

SURPRISING BUT TRUE
QUARTER POUNDERS ARE HEALTHIER THAN BAGELS!

Consult this chart to see how a bagel compares nutritionally to a Quarter Pounder.

	Calories	Protein	Carbohydrate	Fat
Bagel with 2 Tbsp butter	500	11 g	60 g	26 g
Quarter Pounder	430	23 g	38g	21 g

Note: Figures are rounded.

SOURCES: http://www.whatsabagel.com/html/nutrition_facts/bagel_plain.html
http://www.mcdonalds.com/app_controller.nutrition.item.6.html

---

finished last did it in 29:55:56 at a 17:58 pace. Geez, it's hard enough studying for an exam for 4 hours or watching reruns of *Friends* for 2 hours, much less "running" for 16 hours.

So what's the point? It's not to get you to give up your hopes of training for an ultra marathon some day, if that's really your goal. A lot of female runners, however, train as if they were planning to run an ultra marathon when they are really planning to race 1 mile or 5-K. Many female runners eat too little and run far too much! Unless you're training for a 100-mile race, there's no need to put in more mileage for the sake of saying you did more miles. These so-called junk miles are just that, junk! You'll end up running like a junk car ready for demolition. Some scientists refer to this as being overtrained.

A good friend of ours described overtraining as the terrible trio of eating too little, exercising too much, and resting too little. If you're guilty of any of the three, you're setting yourself up for big trouble: chronic injuries, poor performance, insomnia, poor grades at school or poor work performance, and overall grumpiness. So resist the urge to jog a few more easy miles just to add them to your weekly average. (Your training and eating program should involve a systematic progression, not some haphazard, New Age method.)

don't . . . dwell on a bad race

Everyone has a bad race every once in a while. Even if your time in the 5000 was 20 seconds slower than last week, get over it. You need to look at your running progress as a jagged line that trends toward faster times. For instance, "Charting Your Progress" below shows a hypothetical progression of a runner's 5-K race times over a 3-month period. It is expected that your race time may actually get worse during some weeks, but don't fret. The overall trend is what's important. For instance, your week 12 time should definitely be faster than your week 1 time (assuming you are healthy and injury-free). If you aren't improving as an overall trend, however, it's time you sit down with your coach and reevaluate your training program. We'd also suggest you consult with a sports nutritionist as well.

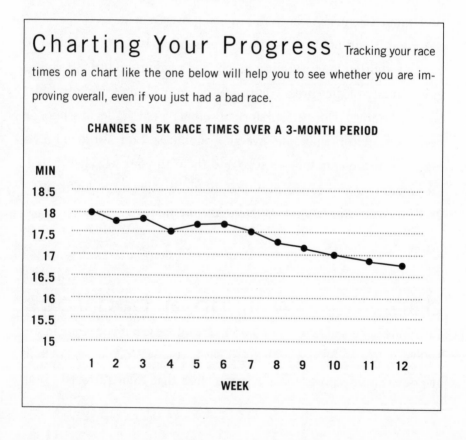

Charting Your Progress Tracking your race

times on a chart like the one below will help you to see whether you are improving overall, even if you just had a bad race.

CHANGES IN 5K RACE TIMES OVER A 3-MONTH PERIOD

don't . . . obsess over a certain number

If you get upset over your body weight, then don't weigh yourself. Obsessing over a 1- to 2-pound change in body weight is like worrying about getting sand on your toes while vacationing in the Florida Keys. It happens! Your weight may fluctuate for many reasons, some of them beneficial. For example, as you taper your training for a big race, your muscles will fill up with stored carbohydrate, which may make you heavier on the scale. Yet, you'll need this carbohydrate on race day, so don't sweat it.

Some women get so upset by a slight gain in body weight that they try to make up for it by running more. This counterproductive mindset is one of the fastest ways to get yourself injured or overtrained. The purpose of training is not for you to lose weight. Your focus should be on performance. Let your body weight take care of itself. If you're

---

Top Ten Dos and Don'ts

Follow these dos and don'ts for optimum success on the track and trails.

1. Do educate yourself.
2. Do eat dairy and meat.
3. Do eat fat.
4. Do eat immediately after training or racing.
5. Don't eat like a POW.
6. Don't treat bagels as a health food.
7. Don't train for the Western States 100-mile race when you'll be racing the 1-mile race.
8. Don't dwell on a bad race.
9. Don't obsess over a certain number.
10. Don't run "just to run."

---

training smart and eating healthy, your body weight will reach its ideal level without artificial prodding.

don't . . . run "just to run" Junk the junk miles. Don't run because you're bored. Don't run just to say you did 50 miles this week. On those days when you're doing junk miles, your body would be much better off resting. For instance, let's say your best friend and fellow cross-country runner asks you to go out for an easy 6-miler on a beautiful Sunday morning in Vermont. Granted, it's a great way to view the foliage, but it's a terrible way to treat your body, especially if this run wasn't planned. Here are better alternatives if you *must* exercise. Get on a bicycle and pedal leisurely through the countryside, or go to the gym and get on the recumbent bike, elliptical trainer, or stairclimber. Each of these exercise machines has less impact on your joints than running, and will give your joints and running muscles a much needed rest. Your best strategy on your unplanned workout days is to stay home and rest. Catch up on studying, your job, or a good book, or treat yourself to a movie.

CHAPTER 6

The Three Amigos never underestimate the importance of exercise, rest, and food

Those who train smart, eat clean, and rest properly are the ones who perform at their best! It seems intuitive that you need to take care of these three basic athletic needs, but it never ceases to amaze us how many runners fail to do so. Too often, runners approach training with excitement and enthusiasm, yet treat rest and diet as mere afterthoughts.

Exercise, rest, and proper nutrition are as interdependent as the wheels on a tricycle. Lose any wheel and the tricycle doesn't travel as smoothly or quickly—if it travels at all! It's the same with your running. Let's take a look at the importance of each of these training components, along with the facts you need to properly incorporate them into your training regimen.

the importance of exercise Obviously, exercise is important. You can eat the most healthy diet and rest properly, but without actual training, you're like a boat sitting in dry dock. To train at your best, you must follow the following golden training principles.

Principle of Specificity. Some exercise physiologists call this the SAID principle, which stands for "Specific Adaptations to Imposed Demands." What this means is that if you want to enhance your distance-running performance, you need to focus your training on the specific muscles and energy systems used in the event. It also means that you need to tailor your diet to meet the demands of the sport. For example, if you compete at the 10,000-meter distance, your training should focus on longer runs and longer speed intervals. Compare this to training for the 100-meter sprint. A sprinter would be wasting her time doing runs greater than 400 meters. On the other hand, the 10,000-meter runner would be wasting her time doing 10- to 20-yard sprints. Your body makes specific adaptations to the exercise stress placed upon it.

On the other hand, this doesn't mean that any nonrunning-type exercise is worthless. There is some evidence that weight training, plyometric drills, and some types of sprint work may help enhance distance-running performance. That said, nonrunning training should not be the cornerstone of your training program.

Principle of Overload. To run faster, you need to train progressively harder. You need to progressively overload the body such that it adapts to the training regimen and gets stronger as a result. In beginning runners, changes in performance come quickly. Just by mere increases in distance run per week, the beginner will experience gains in performance. The trained high school, collegiate, or recreational runner, however, will find that the nature of the exercise overload becomes a little bit more complicated.

Merely increasing mileage may not necessarily translate into faster times; in fact, it may result in injury. This is where the issue of quality versus quantity of training comes into play. This is also where you (or your coach) need to approach your training plan in a systematic or scientific manner. You may need lactate threshold training, plyometric drills, and various interval/speed training to enhance performance without compromising your health. You'll learn more about these specific types of workouts in upcoming chapters.

Principle of Individuality. This principle states that each female athlete will respond to training in her own way. Some runners respond well to long slow distance (LSD), whereas others respond best to interval work or speed training. Clearly, genetics plays a role. This is where the "art" of training comes into play. You must not only master the principles of overload and specificity, but also apply them to your unique physiology, to achieve the best results.

Principle of Detraining. This principle states that if you cease training, your body will revert back to an untrained state. This doesn't mean you should never take a few weeks off. To the contrary, rest (as we'll explain shortly) is important to a successful training program. For instance, taking a month off from running may give your body a much needed rest. In fact, scientists now know that it takes 2 weeks of complete bed rest before the body begins to detrain. Add in some cross-training in the form of walking, cycling, or some other alternate activity to running, and you can preserve your fitness for a month or longer while you simultaneously give your running muscles and mind the rest they need.

the importance of rest

Many runners act as if they are completely allergic to taking a day off. Running is probably one of the more addictive exercises. Let's face it, you feel good after finishing a hard 8-mile run. Those endorphins are coursing through your body faster than stock cars at a NASCAR race, giving you that beloved "runners high." Still, that's no reason to ignore the rest your body needs.

Rest means more than just taking 1 day off a week. To get adequate rest, you should also take a couple weeks off after the track, cross-country, or road-racing season. This rest will give you a mental break. Also, your normal physiology can be restored. Your muscles can completely heal from the wear and tear of the season, and your immune system can get a break from the daily beating it gets from hard running. Giving your immune system a break also means that if you're sick with the flu, it's best you lie in bed, not go out for a run!

So many runners are chronically overtrained because they haven't learned the value of rest. If you're addicted to movement, we have a solution for you. It's called active rest, or nonrunning exercise. Preferably, active rest includes activities that are recreational in nature, such as rollerblading, hiking, or swimming leisurely at the lake or beach. For instance, let's say you recently finished the cross-country season and you're just dead tired. Your legs feel like they've been through a meat grinder. Your body is telling you to rest. Mentally, however, you can't stand the thought of sitting on your rear for a couple weeks. Well, an alternative is active rest. Go to the gym and get on the recumbent bike, elliptical trainer, or stairclimber. Try a yoga or Pilates class. Start that weight-training program that your strength and conditioning coach has been bugging you about. Either way, you're getting some exercise, but you're also giving your running muscles a rest, and your mind a break from the monotony of running. This may also be a good thing to do every once in a while during the competitive season.

the importance of eating clean

For many years, runners and carbohydrates went together like chocolate and peanut butter. Indeed, at the refreshment tables at the end of any major road race, you will find many carbohydrate treats, from bananas to bagels. Although you do need some carbohydrate to provide energy to your running muscles, there's more to eating than loading up on carbohydrates.

Granted, carbohydrates play an important role. Stored carbohydrate in your body serves as your primary fuel source for long-distance events. That said, you can leave the carbo-loading to marathon runners. If you compete in the 1500-, 3000-, 5000-, or even 10,000-meter distance, there is no compelling need to load up on carbs. Yet, simply eating any old carbohydrate you want isn't going to improve your performance.

To run faster, you must eat clean. That means the foods you eat should consist primarily of lean proteins, unprocessed and high-fiber carbohydrate, as well as unsaturated fats. In terms of carbohydrate, you should be aiming for foods that are high in fiber, low on the glycemic index, and minimally processed. In other words, fruits, vegetables, and whole grains are better than white bread, crackers, bagels, and candy. The only times you need carbohydrates that are high on the glycemic index are immediately before a race and immediately after a race or workout.

SURPRISING BUT TRUE
DRINK PLENTY OF FLUID AND BURN FAT!

Water accounts for up to 75 percent of the weight of muscle and plays a role in every chemical reaction in your body. Increasing the volume of fluid in your body, known as body volumization, increases whole-body lipolysis, or fat breakdown.

According to Swiss scientists, body volumization may have some merit with regard to fat burning. In this study, they induced a condition called hypoosomolality in seven healthy young men. Let's say 50 percent of your body is made up of salt. If you were to drink a solution that contained more than 50 percent salt, you'd increase your hyperosmolality. On the other hand, if you were to drink a solution that contained less salt than your body (a 30-percent salt solution), you'd induce hypoosmolality. In essence, you'd be making your body more dilute.

To induce hypoosmolality, subjects were given desmopressin (a drug that makes you retain water) at 8:00 P.M., and then they consumed 2.5 to 3 liters of tap water over the course of the night. The next morning, they again took the desmopressin followed by the intravenous infusion of 0.45 percent salt water at a rate of 200 milliliters per hour for 4½ hours (about 1,000 milliliters total). The researchers then measured glycerol rate of appearance (Ra), a measure of fat burning. They found that subjects had a higher Ra and therefore burned more fat. Furthermore, the increase in fat burning was not associated with changes in any of the lipolytic hormones (such as epinephrine or norepinephrine). According to of the study, " . . . the decrease in osmolality was of a degree frequently observed in clinical conditions, the findings may indicate a role for osmolality in the regulation of lipid, glucose, and protein metabolism. . . . "

What this means is that drinking 8 to 12 ounces of water or a flavored low-calorie beverage every 2 to 3 hours during the day is good for you!

The eating clean concept also applies to protein. Shoot for lean sources of protein—skinless chicken breast, fish (this has good fats!), fat-free milk, low-fat cottage cheese, and an assortment of protein powders that you can find at your local health food store. The same goes for fat. The kinds of fat you need to eat are primarily unsaturated. Fish fat is the best source of fat. Fat from nuts (such as almonds and cashews) and from legumes (peanuts) are good sources. Don't skimp on healthy fats or lean proteins.

Treat your eating program the same way you treat your running program. It should be systematic, sensible, and geared toward improving your recovery and, ultimately, your performance.

CHAPTER 7

The Female Athlete Triad
an overview of
disordered eating
by Chris Lydon, M.D.

Over the past 30 years, the number of girls and women involved in competitive sports has increased dramatically. Today, adolescent girls make up the fastest growing segment of the school-age population participating in organized athletics. For many adolescent girls and young women, this trend spells nothing but good. Sports teach leadership, encourage teamwork, and foster independence. Research shows that girls and young women who participate in organized athletics have better body images, higher self-esteem, and more confidence than their nonathlete, age-matched peers. They are also less likely to smoke, drink, abuse drugs, and engage in risky sexual practices at a young age. And they are more apt to do well in school and pursue higher education. Every imaginable indicator seems to attest that girls who play sports are better equipped to overcome the physical, psychological, and emotional obstacles of adolescence.

Why then do so many of these young athletes succumb to eating disorders? Female athletes are, in fact, three to six times more likely to engage in dangerous eating behaviors than their nonathletic counterparts, and at the college level, their risk for developing amenorrhea (no menstrual periods) is as much as 10 times greater. The irreversible mineral erosion resulting from even brief periods of amenorrhea can strip the athlete of the bone density she will need to last through her adulthood, and predispose her to osteoporosis before her thirtieth birthday.

the female athlete triad The term *female athlete triad* was first coined in 1992. It describes the terrible trio of:

1. Disordered eating (commonly linked to compulsive exercising)
2. Amenorrhea (loss of menstruation)
3. Osteoporosis (bone loss)

Although there are many theories to explain the alarming incidence of this syndrome among young female athletes, most experts agree that eating disorders (which include exercise bulimia) represent poor coping mechanisms. In effect, the compulsive behaviors provide a comforting routine, a means by which a young girl can gain control over what she perceives to be an overwhelming or unpredictable existence.

Although the exact prevalence of the female athlete triad is unknown, studies have reported dangerous eating behavior in 16 to 72 percent of female college athletes, compared with only 5 to 10 percent of women in the general population. Amenorrhea occurs in 4 to 62 percent of female athletes, compared with only 2 to 5 percent of women in the general population. Which brings us back to the question, why is this trend so much more rampant among athletes than nonathletes?

Before we ask ourselves this question, we need to examine what predisposes certain young women to adopt disordered eating patterns in the first place.

how disordered eating begins

Although there is no simple formula to determine who will adopt harmful eating or exercise habits, there are a handful of personality traits that occur with greater frequency among victims of eating disorders. For instance, many women who fall victim to disordered eating tend to be overachievers and perfectionists. Many are highly motivated, self-reliant young women who demonstrate extreme dedication to school, career, and athletics. Unfortunately, any insecurities they might

Traits of Women with Disordered Eating

Women who develop disordered eating tend to have similar personalities. Below are some of the traits disordered eaters tend to share.

- Overachieving
- Perfectionistic
- Highly motivated
- Self-reliant
- Extremely dedicated

have are fueled by the overwhelming prospect of striving to meet lofty (and commonly self-imposed) expectations.

In some instances, emotional trauma can be the cause. It is well-documented that families of anorexics and bulimics exhibit higher-than-normal rates of substance abuse, sexual abuse, and intrusive parenting. Further research suggests a strong genetic component to eating disorders. For instance, women with a first-degree relative who suffers from anorexia nervosa are 12 times more likely to develop anorexia, and 4 times more likely to develop bulimia.

However powerful these influences may be, they are only part of a complex picture that is linked to our current sociocultural climate. A quick study of popular magazines, films, television, and music videos proves that Western culture is obsessed with appearances. And not just any appearance. Young women are constantly bombarded with perverse images of "beauty" in the form of unattainable thinness. Today's runway models are more than 20 pounds lighter than their counterparts of 40 years ago, and most female movie stars are medically underweight. To an impressionable young girl struggling with emotional conflict, the message that thinness equals success can be irresistibly alluring.

Like any eating disorder, the causes of female athlete triad vary, and no two cases are exactly alike. However, athletes do share common at-tributes that may not be present in their nonathletic peers. For ex-ample, girls who are most attracted to competitive sports are likely to exhibit competitive personality traits. According to at least one popular behavioral model, competitive incentive commonly stems from a de-sire for acceptance or praise by a group or individual. For a young woman who responds strongly to this type of motivation, her sense of achievement and success may rely heavily on external sources. For an emotionally vulnerable adolescent, callous remarks and criticisms about body weight could have devastating consequences. Likewise, domineering coaches and overzealous parents may cause athletes to feel stripped of control. To regain a sense of self-command, some athletes feel compelled to adopt excessive exercise habits or severely regiment their food intake.

The good news is that in today's world a large variety of sports are accessible to girls and women. And the status of women's athletics continues to elevate with every passing season. Unfortunately, as the stakes are raised, it appears that the need for girls to excel in the athletic arena also increases. The pressure to win at all costs is no longer confined to elite or even college athletics. This is perhaps best illustrated by the fact that anabolic steroid use by teenage girls has nearly doubled since 1991, whereas steroid use by teenage boys remains unchanged. Moreover, it is a well-known fact that steroid abuse in females contributes to bone erosion and can hasten osteoporotic changes. So, it seems accurate to conclude that steroid abuse is both a cause and a symptom of the female athlete triad.

who is at risk? Although research indicates that female athletes from all sports are at risk for developing female athlete triad, girls and women who participate in certain sports are especially vulnerable. These "high-risk" sports include those where performance is subjectively judged, sports where athletes wear revealing clothing, and sports with weight categories.

Ironically, the most likely candidates for the triad often demonstrate characteristics most prized by coaches. These are the girls who display intense commitment, and train longer and harder than what is required. They may be perfectionists when it comes to technique and highly critical of their own personal performance. Of course, extreme dedication does not necessarily equate with illness. However, the prevalence of the triad suggests that there is sometimes a fine line between healthy enthusiasm and dangerous obsession.

the warning signs There are numerous warning signs for female athlete triad. Although the psychological red flags aren't always easy to notice, the physical signs tend to be more obvious. Those who have the best chance to recognize the triad in its early

---

Sports Where Disordered Eating Is Common

Women involved in the following sports are particularly vulnerable to developing an eating disorder.

- Dance
- Volleyball
- Figure skating
- Basketball
- Diving
- Swimming
- Gymnastics
- Track and field
- Cheerleading
- Wrestling
- Bodybuilding
- Weight lifting
- Aerobics
- Powerlifting
- Distance running
- Rowing
- Distance cycling
- Martial arts
- Cross-country skiing

---

stages are usually coaches, trainers, and parents, people who are closest to the athlete. The trick is to be aware of the warning signs and intervene as early as possible. Some of the warning signs are listed below.

Of course, the behavioral manifestations of disordered eating are typically subtle. Whether you're a coach, trainer, parent, or a running buddy or friend, it is imperative for you to be aware of the warning signs. For coaches, road trips are an especially good time to observe an athlete's eating habits. Here are some more suspicious behaviors you should watch for.

Psychological and Physical Symptoms of the Triad

If you know someone who displays the following symptoms, she may have the female athlete triad.

- Unusual fatigue
- Moodiness
- Peculiar energy fluctuations
- Impaired concentration
- Depression
- Dry hair and skin
- Cold hands and feet
- Fine hair on the face and body (indicating malnutrition)
- Puffy or bloodshot eyes
- Scarring over the knuckles
- Eroded tooth enamel
- Frequent or repeat injuries
- Unexplained weight loss/fluctuations
- Stress fractures
- Amenorrhea

- Being preoccupied with food intake and making odd comments about eating.
- Making frequent visits to the bathroom, especially after meals.
- Eating alone, and hoarding or hiding food.
- Moving food around the plate without eating much.
- Insisting on being fat, even if thin or average.
- Eating abnormally large portions, yet remaining thin or even losing weight.

If you suspect that your fellow running partner or athlete has disordered eating, clearly you should inform her parents or loved ones. Remember, however, that every case is different. Parents should seek the advice of a qualified health professional, such as a family doctor. Your doctor will likely refer you to an individual or organization specializing in the diagnosis and treatment of eating disorders. Depending on the specific situation, this expert will be able to guide you as to the best course of action.

long-term effects of female athlete triad
Whatever the psychobiological and sociocultural forces at work, intense exercise combined with inadequate nutrition eventually leads to dysregulation of the hypothalamic-pituitary-ovarian (HPO) axis, the physiologic connection between your brain and your reproductive system. This results in amenorrhea and decreased estrogen levels. This, in turn leads to decreased bone mineral density, osteopenia (a precurser to osteoporosis), and ultimately osteo-

porosis. Several studies show that the average age of peak bone mass occurs between ages 18 and 25, about 5 years younger than was previously believed. Loss in mineral density or failure to reach optimal bone mass during these crucial years has a permanent effect on skeletal strength. It also places young athletes at higher risk for long-bone injuries, stress fractures, and the spinal compression and hip fractures more commonly seen in older women. What's more, many young women suffer long-term psychological aftereffects and serious medical complications as a result of eating disorders.

Many recovering anorexics, for example, spend months or even years experimenting with extreme food habits before adopting a healthier perspective. It isn't uncommon for the recovering anorexic to experience wide swings in weight, some even going on to develop bulimia. The long-term prognosis can be grim. Although an estimated 40 to 45 percent of anorexics do recover completely, about one-fourth suffer a chronic downhill course. The mortality rate for anorexia is the highest of any psychiatric disorder, with between 10 and 15 percent of anorexics eventually succumbing to starvation, suicide, or serious medical complications brought on by their illness. And, although bulimia is rarely fatal, a full recovery happens in only about half of cases. Nearly one-third of bulimics maintain a "nonspecified eating disorder," and one-fourth of "recovered" bulimics retain some abnormal eating habits.

how to help
The only 100-percent-effective way to "cure" female athlete triad is to prevent it from happening in the first place. For this reason, educating female athletes about the dangers of

disordered eating, excessive exercise, and steroid abuse should be a mandatory component of every sports program that involves young women. Educating your daughters, sisters, and girlfriends about proper nutrition is also vital.

If you suspect someone you know may be suffering from disordered

(continued on page 92)

Female Athlete Triad Defined

Female athlete triad is an unnecessary tragedy, an ugly blemish on the otherwise radiant face of women's athletics. Halting this epidemic is a collaborative effort among coaches, trainers, parents, media, and the athletes themselves. Below are definitions of the triad.

DISORDERED EATING

Patients who exhibit *disordered eating* may engage in a wide range of harmful behaviors. The spectrum of behaviors ranges from a preoccupation with body image, to inappropriate dieting, to bingeing and purging, to full-blown disorders such as anorexia and bulimia nervosa.

AMENORRHEA

Primary amenorrhea is defined as the absence of menstruation by age 16 in a girl with secondary sex characteristics. Secondary amenorrhea involves the loss of menstruation for three or more consecutive cycles in a female with previously regular menses. Amenorrhea is characterized by low blood estrogen levels, and estrogen plays an important role in calcium absorption, which in turn helps to ensure adequate calcium for bone growth and maintenance. Contrary to popular opinion, just because amenorrhea is common among female athletes, it is *not* a normal consequence of training, and should *always* be evaluated by the team doctor or another qualified health professional.

OSTEOPOROSIS

Osteoporosis is defined as the loss of bone mineral density and the inadequate formation of bone. Osteoporosis leads to increased bone fragility and fracture risk. The premature osteoporosis of female athlete triad puts the athlete at risk for stress fractures as well as more devastating fractures involving the hip, pelvis, and vertebral column. The morbidity associated with osteoporosis is significant, and lost bone density can be permanent.

Where to Turn for Help

If you suspect someone you know is suffering from an eating disorder, consult a qualified health professional, such as your family doctor. Also, there are several organizations from which you can seek counsel (listed below).

Academy for Eating Disorders
McLean, VA
Phone: (703) 556-9222

American Anorexia/Bulimia Association, Inc.
New York, NY
Phone: (212) 575-6200

Anorexia Nervosa and Related Eating Disorders, Inc.
Eugene, OR
Phone: (503) 344-1144.

British Columbia Eating Disorders Association
Victoria, BC
Phone: (250) 383-2755

Bulimia/Anorexia Nervosa Association
Windsor, ON
Phone: (519) 253-7421

Eating Disorder Action Group
Dartmouth, NS
Phone: (902) 469-0650

Eating Disorder Education Organization
Edmonton, AB
Phone: (780) 944-2864
www.edeo.org

Eating Disorder Referral and Information
Del Mar, CA
Phone: (858) 481-1515

Eating Disorders & Education Network (EDEN)
Ann Arbor, MI
Phone: (734) 945-3003

Eating Disorders Association of Manitoba
Winnipeg, MB
Phone: (204) 275-3732

Foundation for Education about Eating Disorders (FEED)
Baltimore, MD
Phone: (410) 467-0603

Massachusetts Eating Disorders Association, Inc. (MEDA)
Newton, MA
Phone: (617) 558-1881

National Anorexia Aid Society (NAAS)
Columbus, OH
Phone: (614) 436-1112

National Association of Anorexia Nervosa and Associated Disorders (ANAD)
Highland Park, IL
Phone: (847) 831-3438

National Eating Disorder Information Center (NEDIC)
Phone: 1-866-NEDIC-20
www.nedic.ca

National Eating Disorder Information Centre (NEDIC)
Toronto, ON
Phone: (416)-340-4156

National Eating Disorders Association
Seattle, WA
Phone: (206) 382-3587

National Eating Disorders Organization (NEDO)
Tulsa, OK
Phone: (918) 481-4044

Overeaters Anonymous
Rio Rancho, NM
Phone: (505) 891-2664

Rader Programs, Inc.
Based in California
U.S. & Canada: (800) 255-1818
www.raderprograms.com

St. Louis Behavioral Medicine Institute
St. Louis, MO
Phone: (314) 534-0200

Support and Assistance For Binge Related Eating & Associated Disorders
(SABRE)
Ft. Walton Beach, FL
Phone: (888) 705-6683

eating, you'll want to reach them as soon as possible. An excellent way to do this is to have them speak to an eating disorders survivor, especially if the survivor is young. Quite naturally, adolescents react more favorably to their own peers.

By the same token, as a coach or trainer, you have a responsibility to avoid training tactics that push susceptible athletes over the edge. For example, always praise optimal health, strength, and performance over thinness and body weight. If you must use weight monitoring, do so privately. Requiring weigh-ins for the entire team or singling out individual athletes for weigh-ins is inappropriate, as is imposing consequences for weight gain. If you're a coach, allow the team doctors, nutritionist, or athletic trainer to monitor body composition and weight, rather than yourself.

Finally, whether you're a coach, a mom, a teacher, or a friend, you need to assess the message you're sending to impressionable young athletes. It is important to remind all young women that there is more to sports than winning, and that athletics are about having fun and being physically and mentally healthy.

CHAPTER 8

Overtraining
how to know when you're
doing too much

Have you been feeling chronically tired? Perhaps you can't sleep very well. Then you run, and it feels like you have a 20-pound weight on your shoulders. Your legs feel heavy, as if you are running in knee-deep mud. Perhaps you've even come down with a few more colds. Injuries seem to creep up on you—and stay with you. Worst of all, your times are getting slower. My friend, YOU are OVERTRAINED!

Since it's not obvious to the naked eye, the overtrained state may be difficult to define, but you know when you have it. Unfortunately, too many runners ignore the warning symptoms and try to train through it. They try to "run through the pain" or "run through the tiredness and aches." That's a big mistake!

what is overtraining? In a sense, you might

describe overtraining as a combination of overexercising, undereating, and undersleeping. As prevalent as overtraining may be in distance runners, the solution is so, so simple: Train less, eat more, and get more sleep and rest! According to the leading authorities, there are two phases of overtraining, with one milder and easier to treat than the other. They include:

Overreaching Syndrome. Scientists describe *overreaching* as "an accumulation of training and nontraining stress resulting in a short-term decrement in performance capacity, with or without related physiological or psychological signs and symptoms of overtraining in which restoration of performance capacity may take from several days to several weeks."

Got This? You May Be Overtrained!

If you have the following symptoms, you may be overtrained.

- Slower running times
- Insomnia
- Fatigue
- Achy joints
- Lack of motivation
- Frequent colds or flu
- Lack of energy
- Poor recovery after workouts
- Poor concentration
- Headaches
- General lethargy
- Chronic injuries that won't heal

Overtraining. Scientists describe *overtraining* as "an accumulation of training and nontraining stress resulting in long-term decrement in performance capacity, with or without related physiological or psychological signs and symptoms of overtraining in which restoration of performance capacity may take several weeks to months."

Wow . . . what a mouthful. Here's a more down-to-earth description of it. If you decided to exercise 7 days a week instead of your normal 4 days per week, you'd probably feel sore and tired for 3 to 4 days afterward. That's overreaching. Overtraining is more severe, and would be like never taking any rest days over the course of 4 to 6 months. Believe us, you'd feel pretty burned out eventually. If you exercise too frequently over a period of several months to years, you'll hurt your immune system, your joints will ache, and you'll feel chronically tired and fatigued. That's overtraining.

Simple Solutions to Overtraining

To get back on your feet, try the following remedies.

1. Take a week off from running
2. Bump up your caloric intake. Eat more of everything, including protein, carbs, and fat.
3. When you resume running, consume a protein shake right after you exercise.
4. Try to nap whenever possible.
5. Take a daily multivitamin/multimineral supplement.
6. Take a whey-protein meal-replacement powder once a day.
7. If you still feel tired, take another week off from running and repeat steps 2 to 6.

---

training smart Training smart involves "cycling" or "periodizing" your training, which means you'll need to make systematic alterations in the volume and intensity of your training program. For instance, you could perform high-volume, low-intensity training for a 2- to 3-week period. This could mean easy 7- to 9-mile training runs. You'd follow that period with a 2- to 3-week period in which you bump up your intensity with tempo work, intervals, and hills. This phase could then be followed by a 2- to 3-week period of high-intensity, low-volume training in which you do little slow running and all your miles are quality, high-intensity, high-speed miles. Thus, you're making your body adapt to slightly differing stresses and at the same time avoiding the mental and physical staleness that commonly occurs when runners do the same routine, day in and day out. Suzy trains in this manner. Depending on the time of the year and whether she has an upcoming meet, she'll do different types of training regimens. In chapter 20, you'll find strategies for using the periodization principle.

eating smart Some scientists believe you can prevent overtraining by eating enough calories and getting enough rest. Certainly, food is important. First, you must be getting adequate calories and macronutrients (protein, carbs, and fat). Many female runners do not, possibly because they are operating under the false belief that they must eat very little food to maintain their weight or to lose weight. To get an idea of what a typical female runner needs to eat in a day, consider this: A 130-pound, 20-year-old woman who is 5 feet

7 inches tall and exercises heavily needs about 2,475 calories per day! That's a lot of food. To determine your calorie needs, use one of the many simple formulas available over the Internet. For instance, if you go to this site, you can calculate your caloric needs: http://www.annecollins.com/calories/calorie-needs-women.htm. For more information on which foods to eat, read chapters 11 through 14.

What about supplements? Is there a role for these? The answer is yes. For instance, one might group supplements into three basic categories:

1. Those that act on the central nervous system (brain)
2. Those that act on the immune system
3. Those that act on the musculoskeletal system (muscles, bones, joints).

Let's look at brain supplements first.

supplements for the brain

Doing too much exercise impacts the way our brains function. For instance, some of the most physically and mentally demanding tasks are those undertaken by our military personnel. Sleep deprivation, constant physical work, and bullet-avoidance are things that will definitely put you in a state of fatigue. Certainly, if there is a single group of "athletes" that is severely overtrained, it's military personnel.

The antidote they use for such heavy-duty training? Tyrosine. Tyrosine serves as a precursor to various neurotransmitters, or chemical messengers in the brain, such as dopamine and norepinephrine. Some scientists believe that behavioral changes caused by stress are the result of the depletion of these neurotransmitters. In one study, military personnel who were exposed to 4½ hours of cool temperatures (59°F) and high altitude (2½ to 2¾ miles above sea level) were given either a placebo or tyrosine (100 milligrams per kilogram of body weight). Results showed that tyrosine significantly alleviated such signs and symptoms as headache, coldness, fatigue, sleepiness, and muscular discomfort. In a recent study of a group of military cadets during military combat training, investigators also found that individuals who consumed tyrosine performed better on memory tasks than those that consumed carbohydrate.

supplements for immunity

Overtraining that affects the immune system is the type that most of us associate with a general feeling of malaise and fatigue. Taking a few days off to sit on your lawn chair will help. So will eating certain foods. For instance, whey protein (a protein extracted from milk) is known to positively affect the immune system. Mice fed whey protein have been shown to have a lower incidence of tumors than mice fed either casein or mice-chow. The high levels of the amino acid cysteine found in whey protein are important for glutathione synthesis. This is important because enhanced levels of glutathione benefit the immune system. Other supplements, such as glutamine and arginine, have also been shown to positively affect the immune system. For example, overtrained individuals tend to have low levels of plasma glutamine. Furthermore, athletes who ingest glutamine report fewer infections postexercise versus athletes who don't use glutamine. Glutamine is thought to provide fuel for cells of the immune system. This is perhaps how it keeps you from getting sick.

supplements for the muscles, bones, and joints

You know the feeling, that twinge of pain you feel in your hips or knees after a hard workout. Could your joints be overtrained even though you might otherwise feel fine? Although you may not be suffering from degenerative joint disease (dysfunctional changes in your joints), you may set yourself up for this malady if you don't train smart. In one study performed at Eastern Virginia Medical School in Norfolk, Virginia, scientists gave a combination of glucosamine (1,500 milligrams per day), chondroitan sulfate (1,200 milligrams per day), and manganese ascorbate (228 milligrams per day) to individuals suffering from degenerative joint disease in the knee or low back. After 16 weeks, the participants' knees (but not their spines) showed a significant improvement in osteoarthritic symptoms as demonstrated by the patients' descriptions of the pain, functional questionnaires, and physical examinations.

Both glucosamine and chondroitan sulfate contribute to the structural components (glycoproteins) of our joints. So this combination may be effective for alleviating or perhaps preventing symptoms of degenerative joint disorder.

the big picture
You need to treat your entire body as a system. For instance, even though your muscles and bones may be fine, your immune system might be shot. Or perhaps, you're feeling great, but you have a twinge in your Achilles that just won't go away. In essence, all of these symptoms are related to overtraining. Overtraining is best treated by avoiding it. Bottom line: Training smart results in racing well!

PART 3

How Your Body Runs

CHAPTER 9

How Your Body Makes Energy
the three energy pathways: phosphagen, lactic acid, and aerobic

To run faster and more efficiently, you need to understand how your body produces energy. Once you understand that, you will be better able to understand the right workouts your body needs at the right times to produce successful results. For example, knowing your body's energy systems is similar to a mechanic knowing which fuel to put in which car. Obviously, the engine and fuel of a dragster isn't the same as that of a VW Beetle. The same goes for the human body. For you to achieve success in your running career, you need to be cognizant of the proper fuel your body needs at the proper times. If you aren't, all your training will go to waste.

For the reasons listed above, it's important to understand the three different energy pathways that your body uses to make energy. They are termed the phosphagen, lactic acid, and aerobic energy pathways. Scientists group the first two as the "anaerobic" energy pathways (meaning without oxygen). We'll go over each of these one at a time.

anaerobic energy pathways The

anaerobic energy pathways provide energy for exercise that is intense and short-term in nature (less than 60 seconds). For instance, if you try and sprint once around a quarter-mile track, you'll tap into your anaerobic system. Similarly, if you run a 40-yard dash, you're also using your anaerobic system to power your body. There are two types of anaerobic pathways: the phosphagen pathway and the lactic acid pathway.

the phosphagen pathway

An easy way to understand the phosphagen pathway is to steal an example from the animal kingdom, specifically the cheetah. A cheetah can sprint up to 70 miles per hour, but only for a short time. After its quick sprint, it needs to rest for hours. The American quarter horse is the same way. It can rocket from the starting gate to the finish line in a quarter-mile race, topping out at a speed of 55 miles per hour, but once it's done sprinting it needs prolonged rest to recuperate. These animals run on the phosphagen pathway, meaning they generate energy from stored *adenosine triphosphate (ATP)* and *phosphocreatine (PCr)*. In humans, an all-out sprint will deplete this type of energy pathway in about 10 seconds. So only short-distance sprinters (such as those who run the 40-yard dash) tap into this pathway on a regular basis.

How does this apply to you? Well, unless you want to be a sprinter (and you probably don't, considering you bought this book!), then it would be a waste of time for you to emphasize 40-yard dashes over something like 400- to 800-meter repeats. Remember: It's all about training your body to do what you want it to do. Certainly, running 40-yard dashes will help you run faster in the 40, but such training won't help you in a cross-country race, because these races require the use of a different energy pathway—the aerobic pathway.

lactic acid pathway

The second pathway is the lactic acid pathway. This is the main energy source used for long sprints (400 and 800 meters). If you've ever sprinted all out in the quarter-mile, then you've felt the extreme pain and tightness in your legs as you hit that final turn. Say hello to lactic acid.

Here's how it works. The lactic acid pathway creates energy from the fast breakdown of stored muscle glycogen (stored form of sugar or carbohydrate in your muscles). Anytime you burn glycogen or glucose as fuel, you make lactic acid. It's just a physiologic fact of life. When you sprint, you break down muscle glycogen so quickly that your muscles produce lactic acid as a by-product. The acid buildup causes a drop in muscle pH, and your body is soon forced to slow down. Some of us can metabolize lactic acid quicker than others. If you're in terrific shape, you can metabolize lactic acid faster than someone in bad shape. If you're in poor shape, the lactic acid accumulates and it causes tremendous fatigue. If you don't slow down, you'll fall flat on your face. Again, the 400-meter sprint is the classic example of how the lactic acid pathway functions. However, it isn't the metabolic poison some have called it. On the contrary, it's quite an amazing chemical (see "Lactic Acid: It's all Good!" on page 108).

Part of making yourself a better runner means training your body to run at a faster pace, while simultaneously training your body to produce less lactic acid. By producing less lactic acid, you can run for a longer period without being forced to slow down. Call it lactate threshold training. If you look at some of the best runners in the sports world, their maximum oxygen uptake levels may not differ much at all, but those who can run at a higher lactate threshold speed usually finish first. Higher lactate threshold can work the same way for you. You simply need to train your body to process lactate more efficiently and train your mind to tolerate the pain associated with this type of training.

aerobic pathway The aerobic pathway generates
energy primarily through the aerobic breakdown of carbohydrate and

Where ATP Comes From

Consult the chart below to see the percentage of each energy pathway required for various running events.

PERCENTAGE CONTRIBUTION

Event	Glycogen Phosphocreatine (Phosphagen Energy Pathway)	Glycogen Anaerobic (Lactic Acid Pathway)
100 m	50	50
200 m	25	65
400 m	12.5	62.5
800 m	6	50
1500 m	*	25
5000 m	*	12.5
10,000 m	*	3
26.2 miles	—	—
24-hour race	—	—

*Adapted from McArdle, Katch, and Katch: According to McArdle, Katch, and Katch, PCr will be used for the first few seconds and, if it has been replenished during the race, can be used in the sprint to the finish
Key: "—" means negligible.

fat—that is, it does so "with oxygen." The aerobic pathway is the main energy system used for events that last longer than 1½ minutes (such as the 1500 meters). Once again it's all relative to the distance you're running. Obviously, working on speed (the phosphagen and lactic acid pathways) is more important to the 1500-meter runner than it is to the marathon runner. Generally, runners use some of all pathways at various times.

In this pathway, the body mainly burns stored muscle glycogen and fat for energy. The longer your event, the more you will use fat. Whereas shorter races (such as the 1500 meters) require almost all glycogen, longer events burn more fat. This is good, because your body

PERCENTAGE CONTRIBUTION

Aerobic (muscle glycogen and fat)	Blood Glucose (liver glycogen)	Triglycerides or Fatty Acids
—	—	—
10	—	—
25	—	—
44	—	—
75	—	—
87.5	—	—
97	—	—
75	5	20
10	2	88

Lactic Acid:It's All Good! When it comes

to lactic acid, it isn't all bad. In fact, it's pretty darn important.

In simplest terms, lactic acid is the breakdown product of glucose and glycogen—a process called glycolysis. Basically, lactic acid is a glucose molecule cut in half. Glycolysis can happen so fast (as when you run 400-meter repeats), that the formation of pyruvate (a metabolite of glycolysis) far exceeds the capacity of the mitochondria (the part of the cell that makes energy aerobically) to accept pyruvate and use it to create ATP. So what happens to all of this excess pyruvate? It's converted to lactic acid!

Is it true that lactic acid accumulation gives you the soreness you feel 1 to 2 days after a hard workout? Not really. Scientists have known for at least 20 years that lactic acid has nothing to do with delayed-onset muscle soreness (or DOMS). DOMS is the pain you feel 24 to 72 hours after a hard workout session. It is caused by the tearing of muscle fibers. The lactic acid produced by intense exercise can, however, lead to tired muscles. Thus, when you do some heavy interval work, the immediate pain you feel in your legs is likely the result of lactic acid accumulation (as opposed to DOMS, which is a delayed reaction).

has a nearly endless supply of fat and a limited supply of glycogen. Even so, runners competing in longer events can still hit the wall when they deplete their stored muscle glycogen or become dehydrated.

race time! Let's examine some of the typical distances that

you might run in college or high school. We'll first look at the glamour

Lactic acid buildup during exercise can interfere with muscle contraction, nerve conduction, and energy production, which all lead to tired muscles. That's one reason you fatigue during a fast run. Lactic acid isn't, however, just a useless by-product of energy metabolism. It's also an important energy source. It can be used as an important fuel or as a source for glucose and glycogen synthesis. For instance, when you exercise intensely, lactic acid produced in your fast-twitch fibers can actually go to adjacent slow-twitch fibers and later be used there as fuel. Lactate can also enter the general circulation, where tissues such as the heart, liver, and kidneys can use it as fuel. In fact, about 75 percent of the lactic acid made during exercise is used as fuel, whereas the remaining 25 percent is converted to glucose in the kidney and liver. The removal of accumulated lactic acid helps avert excessively high levels, and the conversion of lactate into glucose helps maintain sufficient levels of blood glucose, an important ingredient for prolonged endurance.

So the next time a so-called expert gives you the laundry list of lactic acid's adverse effects, you can smile to yourself because you know the truth. Lactic acid isn't all that bad.

event of distance running, the mile; or in this case, the "metric" mile (1500 meters).

1500 meters

If you take a look at the chart "Where ATP Comes From," on page 106, you'll see that the 1500-meter event requires 25 percent of its energy from the anaerobic breakdown of glycogen (the lactic acid pathway) and 75 percent from the aerobic breakdown of glycogen.

Since the use of the phosphagen pathway is saved mainly for the sprint to the finish, it would make sense to devote most of your training (75 percent) to aerobic training, such as tempo runs and fartlek (speed play). This doesn't mean you can go out and run slowly for miles and miles, but it does mean that you need to teach your body to run at a faster pace so that it takes you longer to reach your lactate threshold. Conversely, the other 25 percent of your training should consist of anaerobic "speedwork"—that is, training that is faster than race pace. This will teach you to tolerate lactic acid and burn it as fuel. It will also help build leg speed and improve running economy (the amount of oxygen you use when you run).

800 meters

Compare the 1500-meter event with the 800-meter event. In the 800, you need to use equal parts aerobic and anaerobic energy. In this event, you truly need speed *and* endurance! Thus, the 800-meter runner needs to place more emphasis on speedwork and interval training, and less emphasis on aerobic training than the 1500-meter runner.

the marathon and more

As you can see, the 26.2-mile marathon is basically an aerobic event from start to finish. Most of the energy is derived from carbohydrate (glycogen) and fat. So, for the marathoner, there is little need to train the phosphagen pathway. If you're one of those adventure-crazed nuts who yearn to tackle an ultra marathon of 50 miles or more, then you'll be using fat as your main energy source. Training for a 24-hour "race" will make you a very slow runner with lots of endurance.

the big picture Now that you know that training for the 800 meters isn't the same as training for the marathon, keep in mind that great running isn't just about training the right energy pathways. Sure, it's a big part of it, but it isn't everything. There are many elements that need to come together before you can run at your best. For example, new scientific evidence shows that weight lifting can also enhance distance-running performance. How can this be? Although it's true that weight lifting almost exclusively uses the phosphagen and lactic acid pathways, it can improve your running by affecting something unrelated to energy systems. Specifically, it improves your running economy, the amount of oxygen you use when you run. In chapter 19, you'll see how explosive weight training can improve distance running. No kidding.

CHAPTER 10

Muscles
how your heart and skeletal muscles adapt to different kinds of running

Unless your college major is exercise physiology or biology, you may find the following treatise on physiology a wee bit complex. We're going to swim through the plethora of scientific data and present you only the most relevant facts. There are people who dedicate their entire lives to learning how the body adapts to running, and let's face it, if learning the body's physiology were so simple, we'd all be doctors, right? We think it's important you understand the basic physiologic underpinnings of why certain training and nutrition regimens have the effect they do. If you don't have this knowledge, training is like walking blindfolded in a dark room.

We've divided this chapter into little snippets of information dedicated to different aspects of exercise physiology. That way, you can skip those you find to be a yawn and detour over to where you want to be. In brief, the following chapter will cover these concepts:

- Fast- and slow-twitch muscle fibers
- Your heart and exercise
- VO_2 max
- Lactate threshold
- Running economy
- Basic training physiology
- What happens to your body if you've been running for more than 20 years?

fast- and slow-twitch muscle fibers
The difference in physique between distance runners and sprinters is obvious to the naked eye (or naked body, whichever you prefer!). Distance runners, who race at distances from 1500 meters on up, specialize in aerobic performance, and, as a result, run most efficiently with a lean body and just enough muscle to propel themselves at a high speed. A heavier body mass means the runner must work harder to haul these extra pounds over the miles, which is why most elite distance runners are some of the slimmest people you will ever meet. On the other hand, sprinters who compete at the 100- to 400-meter distance are very muscular with very little body fat as well. They need more muscle to power themselves over the short distance. Because they don't have far to go, the weight of their body is not as much of a factor as it is for the distance runner. The 800-meter runner is a hybrid runner who walks the line between being a speed athlete and being an endurance athlete. The physiques of 800-meter runners tend to fall in between that of the sprint athletes and the distance athletes.

These visible differences can be traced to how your muscles adapt to specific types of training. As was discussed in chapter 6, exercise physiologists call this the principle of specificity, or the SAID (specific adaptations to imposed demands) principle. That is, if your goal is to excel at the 3000-meter race, you should focus your training on the metabolic demands of that distance.

Ultimately, how you train your skeletal muscles will determine in large part whether you'll be best suited for running 100 meters or 10,000 meters. That brings us to the concept of muscle fiber types. We're sure you've heard of fast-twitch and slow-twitch muscle fibers. The term *twitch* refers to the speed in which these fibers contract or move. In simple terms, your fast-twitch muscle fibers can be divided into two main types: types IIA and IIB (also called IIX) fibers (see "Muscle Fiber Types"). Your IIA fibers have good endurance and contract quickly. Your IIB fibers contract even faster but have poor endurance. On the other hand, your type I (slow) fibers have good endurance and contract slowly. Most animal and human muscles are evenly split between fast- and slow-twitch fiber types.

For instance, next time you order chicken, you might notice that you have a choice between dark meat (legs) or white meat (breast). Dark-meat chicken contains mainly slow-twitch muscle fibers. The dark color comes from the presence of the red-pigmented cytochrome complexes. The cytochromes are molecules that are found in high amounts in slow-twitch fibers because they are important for promoting aerobic energy production in the muscle. Also, dark meat, or slow-twitch fibers, has lots of mitochondria, also known as the "powerhouse" of the cell, and myoglobin, which is important for storing oxygen. White meat has much less of the cytochrome complexes.

Although most muscles in your body are 50/50 fast and slow, you have certain specialized muscles, such as the soleus (the deeper part of the calf muscle), that are mainly slow, and certain eye muscles that are mainly fast. Furthermore, you are born with a certain muscle fiber type. Training can change some of your fast-twitch muscles to slow-twitch and some of your slow-twitch muscles to fast-twitch, but it can't alter your muscle fiber type in a huge way. So if you're thinking you can suddenly transform yourself into a world-class 100-meter-dash female, think again. Unless your parents are fast, you'll just be spinning your wheels.

the importance of muscle fiber type to your success

If you compete at the extremes of the athletic continuum (for example, you are either a 100-meter sprinter or a marathon runner), then some of your success depends on muscles that contain mainly fast fibers (for sprinting) or slow fibers (for marathon running). That said, muscle fiber type is just one factor out of several that are important for running success. In fact, at the elite level, muscle fiber type is a poor predictor of

---

Muscle Fiber Types As you can see from the graphic below, the slower your muscle fibers contract, the longer they can endure. The faster they contract, the faster you can run, but only for a short period of time.

Type I	Type IIA	Type IIB

slowest <—————————————————————————> fastest

most endurance <—————————————————————————> least endurance

---

who wins and loses. Also, when you race at intermediate distances (such as 1500 meters), muscle fiber type alone is largely unimportant.

What is important is how your muscle fibers adapt to certain kinds of training. For instance, sprint training causes different changes in muscle than endurance training. Thus, you need to make sure you train your muscles in such a way as to maximize their endurance performance. Later in this chapter, you'll see how interval training and long, slow, distance training affect your muscles differently.

exercise and your heart The heart is
an amazing muscle that adapts to running in a profound way. It has many small blood vessels called capillaries, and is loaded with mitochondria, the section of a cell that creates energy, or ATP (adenosine triphosphate). Your heart has tons of this important organelle (about 25 percent of the heart). By the way, your type IIA and I muscle fibers also have lots of mitochondria (about 5 percent of volume), but nowhere near as much as the heart muscle cells.

How does regular running affect the heart? It makes it more efficient! An endurance-trained heart is stronger and pumps more blood per stroke. At rest, most untrained individuals have a heart rate of 70 beats per minute, whereas most trained people have a resting heart rate of less than 50 beats per minute. With each beat, your heart pumps out a certain volume of blood (called the stroke volume). If you multiply your heart rate by your stroke volume, you get a value called cardiac output.

Let's look at the hypothetical scenario of a former couch potato who has been running regularly for 1 year (see "The Exercise Makeover").

As you can see, this runner's heart rate at rest went from 72 to 60 beats per minute, a 17 percent decrease. Her stroke volume increased from 72 to 90 milliliters, a 25 percent increase. As your heart adapts to your training and becomes a more efficient machine, it can pump more blood with fewer heartbeats. One hallmark of endurance training is a dramatic drop in resting heart rate. There have been cross-country skiers with a resting heart rate of less than 30 beats per minute! Suzy's resting heart rate, by the way, is 48 beats per minute.

what your heart does during exercise

During submaximum exercise, such as running at a conversational pace for 30 minutes, an endurance-trained heart works at a lower heart rate

---

The Exercise Makeover

In the chart below, you can see how regular exercise affects the heart rate, stroke volume, and cardiac output of a former couch potato.

	As a couch potato	After 1 year of training	Percent change
HRrest (heart rate)	72 beats per minute	60 beats per minute	−17%
SVrest (stroke volume)	72 milliliters	90 milliliters	+25%
Qrest (cardiac ouput)	5,184 milliliters/ minute	5,700 milliliters/ minute	+10%

Formula: Q (cardiac output) = HR × SV

Before

Qrest = 72 × 72 = 5,184 milliliters per minute, or 5.2 liters per minute

After

Qrest = 60 × 95 = 5,700 milliliters per minute, or 5.7 liters per minute

---

and has a higher stroke volume than the heart of someone who doesn't usually exercise. Thus, cardiac output is the same for both the endurance-trained and untrained person. The trained person, however, works at a lower heart rate. Moreover, perhaps the biggest difference between the trained and untrained heart occurs during maximum exercise (for example, when running a race). Keep in mind, your maximum heart rate is determined by age, which is why we generally figure your maximum heart rate as 220 minus your age.

This, of course, is just a rough estimate. The only true test for determining max heart rate is to perform a max exercise test. During the most common max exercise test, an exercise physiologist would ask you to run on a treadmill in which the speed, the grade, or both are increased every 30 seconds to 2 minutes. Eventually, your body can't perform at the given workload and, hence, you've hit your max.

The average runner can generally use the simple 220 minus the age formula as a gauge of max heart rate. In reality, this formula is within 10 beats, plus or minus, of your true max heart rate. Here's the important point: You cannot change your maximum heart rate. Therefore, the primary way your heart adapts to training is by increasing stroke

---

Determining Max Heart Rate (HRmax)

To figure your maximum heart rate (HRmax), use the simple formula below.

HRmax = 220 – age
Example 1: If you're 20 years old:
HRmax = 220 – 20 = 200 beats per minute
Example 2: If you're 50 years old:
HRmax = 220 – 50 = 170 beats per minute

volume at rest, during low-level exercise, and during maximum exercise. This probably results from two factors:

1. Your heart has a longer diastolic filling time. This means that during the relaxation phase of a heartbeat, your heart can fill up with more blood.

2. Your heart increases the volume of its left ventricle (this is also known as eccentric hypertrophy of the heart). In essence, because the chamber size is bigger, it can therefore hold more blood, and thus pump more blood per beat.

You Get My Drift? Try this experiment. During one of your long runs during the summer, measure your heart rate 10 minutes into the run and again 90 minutes later. You'll notice that even though your running speed is the same, your heart rate is higher later in the run. This increase in heart rate is called cardiovascular drift. As you exercise, you lose fluid via sweat. This fluid comes mainly from your blood volume, so your blood is thicker and more viscous toward the end of the run. With less blood volume, your stroke volume will start to decrease, as it's harder for your heart to pump thicker blood than more watery blood. To allow you to run at the same pace and thus maintain the same cardiac output (and you thought all that physiology was a waste of time), your body compensates for the drop in stroke volume by increasing your heart rate. This is one of many reasons why drinking fluid during a long run is important. You can also experience cardiovascular drift as your muscle fibers start to run out of glycogen and begin to fatigue. As a result, your brain starts to recruit new muscle fibers to do some of the work. After recruiting more muscle fibers, your body then needs to jack up its heart rate to help support these working muscle fibers.

---

max VO$_2$ Max VO$_2$, or maximum oxygen uptake, is a measure of how much oxygen your body can consume each minute during maximum exercise. As exercise intensity goes up, oxygen uptake also goes up. Although there's an upper limit to your max VO$_2$, you can improve it. Your max VO$_2$ is determined mainly by two things: cardiac output and the oxidative capacity of your skeletal muscles. Basically, your heart works to deliver oxygen to working muscles and then your muscles extract oxygen and use it to make energy (ATP). So, to improve your max VO$_2$, you must improve cardiac output as well as the ability of your muscle fibers to extract oxygen. That's where different kinds of training come into play.

Max VO$_2$ is specific to the kinds of exercise you perform. For instance, a cyclist would have a higher max VO$_2$ on a bike test than a runner. On the other hand, a runner would leave a cyclist in the dust if the max VO$_2$ test were done on a treadmill. In another example, swimmers wouldn't do so well on a treadmill max VO$_2$ test, but if you put them in a swimming flume (a water treadmill), they'd kick major tail. This is because each test is specific to the muscles trained. For instance, if you swim regularly, you probably would do poorly on an exercise test that stressed mainly your legs.

Max VO$_2$ is typically measured in volume of oxygen consumed per kilogram body weight per minute (ml/kg/min). Thus, a well-trained female distance runner might have a max VO$_2$ of 65 ml/kg/min, whereas a female couch potato would have a value in the 40s. Many world-class endurance athletes have values in the 70s or even 80s!

Now the ironic thing about max VO$_2$ is that when all is said and done, it isn't that important. Let's explain. If you take someone who has never ran a day in her life and put her on a training program, her max VO_2 will increase in just 1 week! Why? Because one of the fastest adaptations your body makes is to increase blood volume. Just by having more blood volume, your stroke volume goes up, thus increasing cardiac output (and ultimately max VO_2). After about 6 months of training, changes in max VO_2 level off quite a bit. In fact, it may not change much at all after the first year of training.

Fortunately, there's more to performance than max VO_2. It's true that if you go to a local road race, the person who finishes first probably will have a much higher max VO_2 than the person who finishes in the middle of the pack or in last place. If you studied the top 10 or even 20 finishers, however, you'd find that max VO_2 doesn't well explain who wins. In other words, you could win the race and not have the highest max VO_2 of the front pack. So what else explains performance? Ah ha! That's the million-dollar question. Read on. Let's introduce you to the concept of lactate threshold.

lactate threshold and running economy
Your lactate threshold (LT) is the workload at which you start to get a quick rise in blood lactate. Or, to put it another way, it's when the rate of lactic acid accumulation in your blood exceeds the rate lactic acid is removed from your blood. Some people also call this point your OBLA (onset of blood lactate accumulation). Regular training trains your muscles to produce less lactic acid and clear the lactic acid they do produce much more quickly. So for example, if you

previously hit your LT at a speed of 7 miles per hour, training will allow you to run at 8 miles per hour before you hit your LT. Many top runners have LTs at or above 80 percent of their maximum oxygen uptake (max VO$_2$).

Many scientists think LT is the best predictor of running speed! Yes, the higher your LT, the better you can run. Another interesting performance predictor is running economy or efficiency. Running economy is a measure of how much oxygen you need to breathe in to run at a certain pace. The less oxygen you need to run at a given pace, the better.

Now let's look at what our nerdy friends in science have to say about this. In a study from the journal *Medicine and Science in Sports and Exercise*, scientists concluded that "the speed at lactate threshold (LT) . . . is the best physiological predictor of distance running performance." Other studies have similarly found that LT is highly correlated with running performance, from the 800-meter race to the 3000-meter distance!

In fact, consider this interesting case study of an Olympic runner. A world-class female 3000-meter runner underwent regular checkups from 1991 to 1995. They tested her max VO$_2$, lactate threshold, running economy, and running speed at max VO$_2$. This runner improved her race time by 8 percent between 1991 to 1993 (afterward, her race times stabilized). That's pretty darn good! But get this, her max VO$_2$ actually decreased from 1991 (73 ml/kg/min) to 1993 (66 ml/kg/min); that's a 9.5 percent drop. On the other hand, her speed at lactate threshold improved 20 percent and her running economy improved 10 percent. So this female runner got faster because her LT and running economy improved while her max VO$_2$ decreased.

workouts that influence muscle performance
Variety is the spice of a runner's life. If you do only easy, long, slow, distance training, then you'll become really good at running slow for a long time; conversely, if you're a gung-ho runner who doesn't know anything less than breakneck speed, then you'll end up with burnout and injuries. All runners need a good mix of different workouts to achieve a better race time. Below, you'll find the types of workouts that you should incorporate into your training cycle. (See chapter 20 for more details on the training regimens.)

Downhill running. Running on a gradual decline helps you improve the turnover of your legs. If you are breaking your stride while running, the downhill is too steep.

Fartlek. This Swedish word means "speed play," and that is exactly what you do. Run a total distance of 3 to 6 miles, incorporating surges of various lengths and speeds into your workout over varied terrain. Fartlek teaches your muscles how to handle variations in running speed. This might also improve your lactate threshold.

Hill repeats. Similar to interval training (below), you will use the uphill for the intense part of your workout and the downhill for recovery. Hills are great for building muscular strength in the thighs, which is critical if you compete in hilly cross-country races.

Intervals. During interval training, you will run repeated distances of 200 meters or farther followed by a recovery interval. The length of the run and the length of the recovery interval are determined by the phase of training you are in at the time. Examples of interval workouts include ten 400-meter surges with 90 seconds of recovery, or three 1600-meter surges with 3 minutes of recovery. Intervals improve your ability to remove lactic acid and increase your running speed.

Speed endurance. For these workouts, you will run at race pace or faster for 200 to 1600 meters, taking a full recovery after each repeat. One example of a speed-endurance workout would be three repeats of 600 meters with 8 to 10 minutes recovery. For speed-endurance training, the primary goal is to improve long-term speed.

Speedwork. Similar to interval training, speedwork involves run-

---

Training without Moving Some of your

body's most important muscles are the ones you use to breathe: your diaphragm below your lungs and intercostals between your ribs. Some intriguing but not well-known scientific work has shown that if you train your breathing muscles, your performance can improve. Who said heavy breathing was just for telephone pranksters?

A study from the University of Birmingham in the United Kingdom looked at the effects of "inspiratory muscle training" on time-trial performance in 16 cyclists. If you've never heard of this concept, it's actually fairly simple. It's like weight training, but with your breathing muscles. Think of the effort your breathing muscles feel when you're tired and fatigued. It makes sense that if you trained those muscles to be able to inhale even better with more strength, then you'd be more successful at sports in which oxygen uptake is critical (for example, running). To train their inspiratory muscles, the cyclists used a device called TRAINAIR that allows them to breathe against a resistance. The device is similar to breathing in through a straw (the small hole makes it harder to breathe in). After the training period, cyclists experienced less "effort" when breathing and they improved a simulated time trial at the 20-kilometer and 40-kilometer distances. The makers of TRAINAIR suggest that you train your respiratory muscles three times weekly for at least 8 weeks to see results.

ning short, intense sprints of 50 to 150 meters, followed by a full recovery after the repeats. An example would be 1×50, 1×100, 1×150, 1×150, 1×100, 1×50 with 3 minutes recovery. For short-distance speedwork, the primary effect is the improvement of top running speed.

Tempo running. For these workouts, you will run at a pace 10 to 30 seconds per mile slower than your current 10-K race pace for a distance of 2 to 4 miles. Tempo runs can be run for time or for a set

---

Old Runners Never Die, They Just Trip on Their Shoelaces
Here's a perfect example of why running, by itself, is not good enough to fight the ravages of aging. To see how well consistency affects performance and health, researchers tested more than 100 runners between the late 1960s and the early 1970s. At the time of testing, all runners were well trained and competitive. Over a 22-year span, some runners maintained very high levels of training, whereas others quit running and sought the comfort of their La-Z-Boy recliner.

The runners who continued to train had a drop in max VO_2, but the decline was less than for those who stopped running completely. Running does keep your heart ticking like clockwork, but in the battle against time, time always wins. Also, even though those who kept training gained body fat, those who quit training gained the most fat. Aging runners also lost lean body mass, just not as much as the coach potatoes. So, to keep your health in top shape, you better start spending more time hitting the weights. Bottom line: If you keep running, you'll be a lot better off than someone who quits. If you lift weights, however, you'll be better off than someone who only runs.

number of miles. Tempo running helps prepare your body for running at race pace.

Tempo intervals. A variation of tempo running, tempo intervals involve running repeats of 400 meters to 2 miles, followed by a short recovery of 30 seconds to 2 minutes. The total distance run in your tempo interval session should equal 2 to 4 miles.

Overdistance training. This is your typical long run at an easy-to-moderate pace. It is important for developing a base level of endurance. As you get better trained, however, you should do less overdistance and more quality speed training.

Plyometric training/explosive strength training. Even though this mode of training isn't typically put under the rubric of "endurance-type training," there's scientific evidence that "plyos" can actually improve running economy. Plyos involve high-speed jumping, bounding, or quick sprint drills. (See chapter 19 for more details.)

Put simply, you can really divide each of the above 10 workouts into two broad categories: interval training (such as 400-meter repeats) and "constant" intensity training (such as tempo runs). Now the reason you need to do a mix of both has to do with how your body adapts. Hard interval training makes your heart stronger; on the other hand, hours of continuous running (this could be lactate threshold training or overdistance training) greatly improves the endurance of your muscles. So you get both central adaptation (the heart) and peripheral adaptation (the muscles).

PART 4

Fuel for the Ultimate Runner

CHAPTER 11

Become a Professional Eater
how the concept of eating clean can revolutionize your training

The USDA's Food Guide Pyramid is as useful to runners as an ice cube to an Eskimo. The pyramid, depicted on the sides of cereal boxes, doesn't separate low-fat proteins from high-fat ones, good fats from bad, or carbohydrates that are low on the glycemic index (GI) from those that are high on the index. Instead, it lumps all of these food groups into broad categories, with breads and most carbohydrates forming the pyramid's base, vegetables and fruits forming the next tier up, followed by protein and dairy, and finally, fats and sweets at the top. The idea is to focus your diet on the base of the pyramid and eat sparingly from the top. Interestingly, the so-called science behind the government's food plan for better health is not as exact as you've been led to believe.

For runners, the best eating plan has no resemblance to the pyramid. As you'll soon learn, we recommend you stay away from many of the foods at the pyramid's base and maximize many of the foods at its tip—the complete opposite advice of what the pyramid recommends. In addition, we'll tell you to focus on some of the foods from the protein, carbohydrate, and fat categories—and to avoid others from those very same categories!

So hopefully you are starting to get a clearer picture about why the Food Guide Pyramid may not be the best food plan for you to follow. If you find that surprising, there's more. We'd also like to point out that calories are important but that not all calories are created equally. Yes, believe it or not, eating protein calories versus fat calories versus carbohydrate calories does not result in the same kinds of weight gain or weight loss.

a calorie is not a calorie How often

have you heard this refrain: "If you eat more calories than you expend, you'll gain weight; if you eat fewer calories than you expend, you'll lose weight." To a certain extent that's true; but it's also naïve. It doesn't take into account individual biochemical differences between human beings. For instance, have you ever seen that lucky person who can eat all day and night and can't seem to gain a pound? We call those types "hardgainers." For such people, gaining weight is a difficult proposition. Then you have the type of person who seems to eat nothing but celery sticks and water, yet keeps gaining weight! I guess you might call such people "easygainers." Most of us fall somewhere in the middle of those two extremes.

Also, your body does not treat protein, fat, and carbohydrate calories

equally. To top it off, your body treats different protein sources differently, different carbohydrate sources differently, and different fat
sources differently. In a nutshell, eating fat from peanuts is not the same
as eating fat from a big slab of fried bacon. Just in case you think we're
making this up, here's some food for thought.

If a calorie is just a calorie, it shouldn't matter what you eat, correct?
Wrong. Here are just two compelling studies to prove this point, both
showing that, even if you keep your calorie intake constant, you can
lose more fat by consuming a diet rich in protein compared to a diet
rich in fat.

In one study, scientists asked 20 men to switch from their habitual
diet of 17 percent protein, 47 percent carbohydrate, and 32 percent fat
to a diet that consisted of 30 percent protein, 8 percent carbohydrate,
and 61 percent fat for 6 weeks. Despite the large amount of fat consumed, the low-carb diet resulted in a drop in blood triglyceride levels,
postprandial lipemia (the amount of fat in the blood after eating), and
serum insulin levels. Additionally, levels of the healthy HDL cholesterol increased. The best news of all is that the low-carb diet resulted
in a significant increase in lean body mass, with the men each gaining
2.4 or more pounds of muscle and losing roughly 7.5 pounds of fat. In
these men, a low-carb diet improved blood markers of health, metabolism, and body composition.

Okay, that's a fluke you say. Well, let's look at another study done in
a group of normal young women. These women started out eating an
average of 1959 calories, of which 50 percent came from carbohydrate,
16 percent from protein, and 34 percent from fat. Researchers divided
the women into two groups. For 10 weeks, both groups consumed the
same number of calories; however, one group consumed a diet com-

posed of 41 percent carbohydrate, 30 percent protein, and 29 percent fat, whereas the other group consumed a diet composed of 58 percent carbohydrates, 16 percent protein, and 26 percent fat. If they're eating fewer calories, they should all lose weight, right? Well, yes and no. The carbohydrate group lost a total of 15.3 pounds compared with a 16.6-pound loss in the protein group.

Let's look at the numbers more closely. The carbohydrate group lost 10.4 pounds of fat versus 12.3 pounds of fat in the protein group. Also, the carbohydrate group lost 2.7 pounds of lean body mass compared with a 1.9-pound loss in the protein group. So the protein group lost more weight overall, maintained more muscle, and burned more fat. The protein group also reported greater satiety with their meals.

turning up your digestive furnace

So why would a diet rich in protein burn more body fat than a diet rich in carbohydrates? There are many reasons, but one of them centers on the amount of calories your body burns as it digests the food you eat. When you consume food, any food, your body burns calories simply to digest and absorb your meal, which increases your metabolic rate (the rate at which your body burns calories) after you eat. This is called the thermic effect of food, or the thermogenic effect of feeding. Not all foods affect your thermic furnace the same way. For example, eating 1,000 calories of butter is not treated (energetically) the same as eating 1,000 calories of skinless chicken breast; chicken turns up your furnace about 20 percent more than butter! You can probably lose weight eating 1,500 calories worth of jelly beans, but you'll probably have more fat and less muscle. On the other hand, eating 1,500 calories worth of lean protein, unprocessed carbohydrates, and unsaturated fat food sources will likely induce a healthier kind of weight loss. You'll lose fat, and spare lean body mass, such as muscle and bone.

What's the difference between eating protein, carbohydrates, and fat? In one study, 10 participants ate three different test meals, each having about 557 calories. Each meal contained 68 to 70 percent of either protein, carbohydrates, or fat. Researchers tested the subjects' metabolic rate during the 7-hour period after they ate the high-protein, high-carbohydrate, and high-fat meals. The high-protein meal resulted in a 183 percent greater thermic effect than the high-carbohydrate meal and 169 percent greater thermic effect than the high-fat meal. There was no difference in thermic effect of carbohydrates versus fat. In terms of calories, the high-protein meal had a thermic effect 40 calories greater than fat or carbohydrate. You might think that 40 calories is just a drop in the bucket, until you think about it over the long haul. If you took a 40-calorie difference and multiplied it by 365 days of the year, that translates into a 14,600-calorie difference. A pound of fat equals 3,500 calories. Thus, a 14,600-calorie difference might result in a 4.2-pound loss of fat, just from eating more protein. That's significant, particularly if you're already exercising and are lean.

Interestingly, most of the thermic response to eating protein is accounted for by increases in protein synthesis (such as making new muscle protein). Hence, boosting your protein intake will also help you to recover more quickly after your workouts.

So is a calorie a calorie? Wait. There's more!

What do you think would happen if you put two groups of women on a diet consisting of 1,700 calories but consisting of different types of foods? For example, let's say group A eats more protein and less carbohydrate than group B. Do both groups lose the same amount of weight? Afraid not. The group that eats more protein will lose more body weight and more body fat. At the same time, group A will spare more lean body mass (mostly muscle); eating more protein helps spare lean body mass. Also, your body becomes better at burning fat when you restrict carbohydrate intake. Because the body breaks down protein more slowly than carbohydrate, blood sugar levels will be more stable for group A than group B. There are some who believe that if you can maintain steady levels of blood sugar and insulin and avoid the huge highs and lows (as from eating candy all day), you'll gain less body fat and weight. The bottom line is that what you eat is as important as how many calories you consume. Remember, eating 500 calories worth of popcorn and butter isn't the same as eating 500 calories of grilled tuna, broccoli, and half of a sweet potato.

So is a calorie just a calorie? Certainly not.

why you should *not* follow the USDA food guide pyramid The following is an excerpt from a USDA Web site (http://www.nal.usda.gov/fnic/Fpyr/pyramid.html): "The Pyramid illustrates the research-based food guidance system developed by USDA and supported by the Department of Health and Human Services (HHS). It goes beyond the basic four food groups to help you put the Dietary Guidelines into action. The Pyramid is based on USDA's research on what foods Americans eat, what nutrients are in these foods, and how to make the best food choices for you. The Pyramid and this booklet will help you choose what and how much to eat from each food group to get the nu-

trients you need and not too many calories, or too much fat, saturated fat, cholesterol, sugar, sodium, or alcohol. The Pyramid focuses on fat because most American's diets are too high in fat. Following the Pyramid will help you keep your intake of total fat and saturated fat low. A diet low in fat will reduce your chances of getting certain diseases and help you maintain a healthy weight."

Now if it's supported by the Department of Health and Human Services, then it must be good advice, right? Wrong! First of all, the Food Guide Pyramid was developed in 1992. That's a long time ago, and, even for the average American couch potato, scientists have learned much more about proper nutrition since then. For example, since 1992, scientists have discovered that not all fats are created equally: some fats are good for your health, whereas others can contribute to heart disease and cancer. The same goes for grains and proteins. Some should be maximized in your diet; others should be minimized.

That's just what we know about how couch potatoes should eat. When it comes to fit people such as yourself, the pyramid is an inane and insane piece of dietary advice. Indeed, when it comes to runners (or any athlete), the pyramid's advice is particularly troublesome. Let's start at the top, with the pyramid's advice to eat all fats and oils sparingly.

fats and oils

"The Pyramid focuses on fat because most American's diets are too high in fat." Part of that statement is true, but part of it is misguided. The truth is most American diets are too high in the wrong fats! After all, there are good fats and bad fats.

How can you group all fats and oils together? Healthy fat sources, such as monounsaturated fat (MUFA) and polyunsaturated fat (PUFA), are much better for you than the saturated varieties found in fatty animal products. Trans fats, found in processed foods and commercially baked goods, are downright awful for your health (if you read a label and it says "partially hydrogenated" on it, the food contains trans fats). On the other hand, fat from fish (polyunsaturated) is very healthy for you. The specific fats from fish are called EPA (eicosapentanoic acid) and DHA (docosahexanoic acid). Consumption of EPA and DHA can decrease the risk of heart disease, boost your immunity, and reduce muscle soreness and joint pain. So the fat from fish should not be listed at the tip of the pyramid! Indeed, you should be eating lots of fish. At the minimum, eat about 8 ounces of fatty fish, such as salmon, once per week. Other great choices include cod and tuna.

You should also consume the unsaturated fats (MUFA and PUFA) instead of the saturated fats. Fat from avocados, olives, peanuts, nuts, and other plant foods is good for you. The fat you find in butter, margarine, and certain cuts of beef is bad. Limit your consumption of butter, margarine, whole milk, and fatty cuts of meat. Choose lean sources of animal products, such as fat-free milk, skinless chicken breast, and sirloin.

Sweets, by the way, are also listed at the top of the pyramid, and we do agree that you should eat them sparingly. In fact, any processed, high-GI carbohydrates are just plain poison to an athlete's body because they have little nutritive value. So, if we were constructing our own pyramid, we'd place all empty carbs—sugar, candy, white bread, crackers, pretzels, and Pop-Tarts—at the top. On the government's pyramid, by the way, many of these carbs are listed at the base. That said, there is a time and place for high-GI carbohydrates, such as just before or after a workout when your muscles are primed to convert this type of sugar into stored glycogen or energy.

milk, yogurt, cheese, meat, poultry, fish, dry beans, eggs, and nuts

Now let's take a look at the second tier from the top of the pyramid. Here you have the dairy category and the protein category—or, at least, that's about the best way to describe this bizarre collection of food. This second tier is just absurd. First of all, on the dairy side, it doesn't differentiate between whole milk and fat-free milk. Isn't milk a great source of protein? Shouldn't that be on the protein side? And why are dry beans in this category? For instance, kidney beans are 73 percent carbohydrate and 25 percent protein. Beans belong with the carbohydrates. Then you have nuts. Nuts are a great food source, but they don't belong in the protein category. Peanuts, for example, contain more than 70 percent fat (a healthy fat, by the way) and roughly 14 percent each of protein and carbohydrate. Perhaps peanuts best fit in the fats and oils category.

Now let's look at the meats. First of all, different cuts of beef contain different amounts of artery-clogging saturated fat. Regular ground beef contains roughly 42 percent saturated fat, whereas a sirloin roast contains roughly 34 percent. Chicken contains much less fat if you remove the skin. So, in our minds, it's ludicrous to lump fried chicken in the same category as grilled skinless chicken breast. Fish is an excellent protein source, especially salmon, which also has high levels of healthy fat (EPA and DHA). Eggs are also a great protein source; however, if you want to eliminate some of the saturated fat, egg whites are an excellent alternative to whole eggs. If we were building our own pyramid, we would eliminate these dairy and meat categories in favor of grouping foods into lean proteins versus fatty proteins.

fruits and vegetables

Up until this point, we've ripped apart the Food Guide Pyramid. Now we have something positive to say. You can't eat too many vegetables. On that point, we agree with the Food Guide Pyramid. Fruits are an excellent source of water, vitamins, minerals, antioxidants, and fiber as well. Eat fresh fruit as part of your daily eating plan.

In fact, you can't go wrong here. Fruits and vegetables are full of healthy phytochemicals, which help boost your immune system, keep your cell membranes healthy, and promote longevity!

bread, cereal, rice, and pasta

Now let's take a look at the base of the pyramid, at the foods the pyramid suggests you turn to for the bulk of your dietary choices. Some of the foods listed here are just plain bad for you. As a general rule, you should consume foods that are unprocessed, but the pyramid lists both processed and unprocessed grains and carbohydrates at the base. Scientists have shown that eating a lot of processed, high-GI carbohydrates is by itself a risk factor for promoting cardiovascular disease.

So, even though the pyramid lists white bread at its base, you'd do best to avoid it, opting for whole-grain, high-fiber bread instead. Cereal, also listed at the base, for the most part is processed carbohydrates. It's okay to eat cold cereal from time to time, but choose cereals that contain fiber (for example, bran flakes). Similarly, switch from white rice to brown rice.

Now let's talk about pasta. Contrary to popular opinion among runners, pasta isn't necessarily an ideal carbohydrate source. First of all, it's processed. Second of all, it is one of the most calorically dense foods you can consume. For example, 1 cup of cooked spaghetti contains about 200 calories. Do you know how easy it is to eat 1 cup of cooked pasta? The average individual probably eats four times that much at your typical Italian restaurant. Add the buttered garlic bread, tomato sauce, and salad, and you've consumed as many calories as three Big Macs! Now, if you have a hard time consuming enough calories to maintain your weight, go ahead and eat pasta. Just choose whole-grain varieties, and don't make it your first carbohydrate food choice.

the *fast track* eating plan So now

you know how *not* to eat. Let's talk about how you *should* eat for optimum health, performance, and weight. The overriding philosophy of the *Fast Track* eating plan can be summed up in two important words: Eat Clean. Clean eating is simple: Choose lean sources of protein, unprocessed carbohydrate foods, fats that are healthy, and a variety of fruits and vegetables. You don't need an advanced degree in mathematics to figure out how to eat clean or well. You don't need to count calories, weigh your foods, or find out the calorie, protein, and fat content of every food you eat. Most of us (unless we can afford a personal nutritionist) don't have time for that. Instead, we've made it easy for you by providing you with a list (on page 140) of the "Foods You Should Eat Most of the Time" and the "Foods You Should Limit Most of the Time." You'll notice that we don't recommend you entirely eliminate certain foods. That just isn't practical or very fun.

Seems easy right? Just eat most (about 85 percent) of your foods from the "Foods You Should Eat Most of the Time" category. And if you want to have a cheat day or cheat meal once a week, then go ahead and eat five slices of pizza topped with a bucketful of cheese and down it with your favorite soda or drink. Don't feel guilty about it either. Because *cheating is part of your eating plan* as well. (You'll learn more on the concept of cheat meals later!) Also, keep in mind that there are occasions when you want to eat a sugary, high-GI carbohydrate (such as after your workout). Most of the time, however, opt for the unprocessed, low-GI carbohydrate food sources.

Foods You Should Eat Most of the Time
The bulk of your diet (about 85 percent) should consist of the following foods.

PROTEIN

- Fish (salmon, tuna, and sashimi and other raw fish are great!)
- Eggs (mostly egg whites; but 3–4 whole eggs/week is fine)
- Skinless chicken breast
- Canned tuna
- Milk protein (whey protein, casein protein; seen mainly in protein powders and ready-to-drink protein shakes)
- Fat-free milk
- Lean cuts of beef
- Soy protein (in protein powders or drinks)

CARBOHYDRATE

- Vegetables
- Dry beans
- Whole oatmeal
- Brown rice
- Yams, sweet potatoes
- High-fiber, low-GI fruits

FAT

- Fat from cold-water fish
- Olives and olive oil
- Peanuts, peanut butter, and peanut oil
- Nuts
- Flax oil
- DHA/EPA supplements

the cheat day or cheat meal

Ah ha! This will be your favorite day. Pizza, cheesecake, ice cream, and a bag of chips. Yes, eat these junk foods and don't feel bad about it. It'll give you a break from the monotony of eating clean most of the time. In the *Fast Track* eating plan, you can eat up to five cheat meals a week. You can do this in two ways. You can eat all of your cheat meals on the same day in one giant splurge and then eat clean for the rest of the week, or you can spread your cheat meals out over the course of the week.

Foods You Should Limit Most of the Time
The foods below should make only an occasional appearance on your breakfast, lunch, or dinner plate.

PROTEIN
- Fatty meats
- Lunchmeats
- Whole milk
- Hot dogs

CARBOHYDRATE
- White bread
- Pasta
- White rice
- Most cereals
- Fruit juice
- Bagels
- Sodas with sugar
- Pastries
- Cookies
- Cakes

- Candy
- Crackers
- Pizza
- Desserts
- Any drink that contains calories (for example, beer)
- Anything with lots of sugar
- Anything in a package!

FAT
- Butter
- Margarine
- Fat from fatty meats and lunchmeats
- Fat from fried foods
- Hydrogenated oils or trans fats (seen in lots of packaged goods)
- Ice cream

Let's say you eat 5 meals per day. That totals 35 meals per week. If you had a cheat day on Saturday, that would be 5 cheat meals out of 35 meals for the entire week. Then you'll have to eat like a saint the rest of the week. Many athletes find it easier to have one cheat meal every other day. So that could mean a cheat meal on Monday, Wednesday, Friday, and Sunday. Spreading out your cheat meals over the week may help you psychologically to feel more satisfied and less deprived.

If you're the type of person who is a perfectionist, you might find it hard to have a cheat meal at all. You tell yourself, "I've been eating well and training smart, and my performance is improving. Why should I

How To Be a Professional Eater

If you were attending college on a track scholarship or were a professional runner, you would learn to treat your body as your meal ticket. You would train as if running were your job. Just as putting in time on the track would help you earn the money you need to attend school, so would putting in time in the cafeteria by eating the right foods. Eating is how you fuel your body for your workouts. Part of your *job* as a runner is eating well. You wouldn't fuel up a race car with cheap gas, so why would you fuel up your own body with junk food? Treat your body as if it were a race car. Give it the best fuel.

For instance, you wouldn't show up late for a real job would you? Of course not. So treat eating the same way. Don't skip your meals, especially breakfast. Eat five or six small meals per day. This will ensure that you have a steady stream of fuel (such as carbohydrates and fat) and amino acids (to help repair damaged cells) over the course of the day. Also, research shows that eating frequent small meals is good for lowering cholesterol levels. Grazing is better than gorging. Eat lean protein sources. Eat healthy fats. Eat unprocessed carbohydrates. Eat well, as if your job depended on it!

cheat?" Well the answer is, you don't have to cheat. Psychologically, cheating gives you a mental break from having to be perfect all the time. One cheat meal (or five) per week is *not* going to adversely affect your training or performance. Our advice: have a cheat meal every now and then. Maybe it's not once a week; maybe it's once per month. But do it. You'll be happier for it!

surviving parties and holidays

You're about to go home for the Thanksgiving holiday and you know what your mom has in store for you: unlimited turkey, gravy, buttered rolls, pumpkin pie, desserts, and a veritable smorgasbord of food. Should you pig out and chalk it up as a cheat day or days? Rather than being a party pooper or the one who always has to eat perfectly, enjoy the holidays. If you want a hefty serving of apple pie, go ahead and have it. Thanksgiving is only once a year. Besides, it's the most celebrated day of food gluttony. So celebrate. Before the Thanksgiving holidays, however, make sure that your meals are as clean as a whistle. For instance, if you know that on Thanksgiving weekend you'll be eating nonstop from dusk to dawn, then in the preceding 2 weeks you should refrain from having a cheat day or meal. Eat clean for those 2 weeks knowing that you'll reward yourself when you get home for the Thanksgiving break.

What about parties? Again, depending on what stage of training you are in, you can allow yourself some fun at a party. Go ahead and have chips, soda, and so on. On the days before that, however, eat clean. It's all a matter of balancing when you eat clean and when you cheat. I guess you could live the life of perfection and never cheat. You'll be the lone soul at the dinner table on Thanksgiving insisting that you eat skinless chicken breast with broccoli. You know what? That's no fun.

CHAPTER 12

Protein
the neglected macronutrient

If you're like most runners, you've probably been taught the importance of eating carbohydrates, that you need them for energy. On the other hand, protein has sort of taken a backseat to carbohydrates. In fact, it's our experience that many runners subscribe to the following myths surrounding protein intake.

Myth #1: Protein is bad for your kidneys.

Myth #2: Too much protein is bad for your bones.

Myth #3: Too much protein can cause you to get too big, like a bodybuilder.

None are true. We'd like to let you in on a secret. Of the three major macronutrients (protein, fat, and carbohydrates), only two of them are essential. Meaning, you *need* to consume them as part of your daily diet. Do you know which two? This may surprise you, but carbohydrate doesn't make the list. The two nutrients you need are protein and fat!

Yes, oddly enough, your body does not have a dietary need for carbohydrate. There is no such thing as an essential carbohydrate; however, there are numerous essential amino acids, the building blocks of protein. There are also essential fats or fatty acids. Your body cannot make these amino acids and fats and cannot survive for very long without them. Thus, you need to eat protein and fat! Yet it is these macronutrients that are the most neglected by runners and other endurance athletes. That doesn't mean you should give up carbohydrates. On the contrary, the point we're making is that you also should not neglect your protein and fat intake.

why runners need more protein

You, as a runner, need more protein than the Recommended Dietary Allowance (RDA). Here's why. Your body is made up mainly of two things: protein and water. Proteins are part of your muscles, bones, cells, enzymes, antibodies, blood, organs, and so on. Even though protein primarily provides the required amino acids for maintaining the health of our organs and tissues, the need for this macronutrient is elevated if you're an avid exerciser.

One reason: Recovery! We know some of you might think that you'll get big muscles that'll slow you down. Now, if you quit running and started bodybuilding, then yes, you would get bigger. Running, however, is a catabolic activity. In other words, your body adapts to distance running by getting smaller, not bigger. Smaller and lighter runners tend to be the fastest as well. You need to have healthy muscles to perform at your best. Each time you run, you cause tremendous muscle protein breakdown.

For instance, when was the last time you did repeat strides or speed-work on a downhill incline? You probably became very sore 1 to 2 days afterward, right? Well, that delayed-onset muscle soreness (also known as DOMS) is due to microtears in your muscles. You've literally torn some of your muscle fibers into little bits and pieces. To fix your muscle fibers, you need to give them the building blocks they need for repairs. That's where amino acids and protein come in. Without the protein, you'll have difficulty recovering. Keep in mind that eating carbohydrates facilitates recovery as well; albeit in a different manner. (See chapter 14 for more details on carbohydrates.)

How much protein do you need? Put it this way, mixing rice and beans isn't going to do it! That half glass of fat-free milk in the morning isn't enough either. A cup of fat-free milk has roughly 8 grams of protein. If you're a 120-pound runner, that means you should be drinking 15 cups of fat-free milk to meet your daily protein needs! Now mind you, that's if your only protein source is fat-free milk. Of course, you'll be eating other foods. This gives you an idea, however, of how much you need to consume to meet your daily requirements.

As a runner, you need 1.5 to 2 grams of protein daily per kilogram of body weight. Because most of us don't like working in kilograms, we generally recommend you eat 1 gram of protein per pound of body weight daily. That's slightly higher than the 2 grams per kilogram of body weight a day recommendation, but it's easier to remember. As a general rule, consume a lean protein source 4 to 6 times daily (or every 3 hours). If you don't have time for a real meal, try a protein bar or a meal-replacement shake. It's especially important you consume protein (and carbohydrates) immediately after you run.

Can you overdose on protein? Protein intakes as high as 1.3 grams of protein per pound of body weight have been shown to have no effect on kidney function. In fact, Darryn Willoughby, Ph.D., an associate professor of exercise physiology at Texas Christian University, states that "There's absolutely no evidence that consuming protein at levels greater than the RDA has any harmful effects in normal healthy adults." Another concern is bone health. Does eating a lot of protein compromise your bone mineral content? A study in the journal *Nutrition Reviews* reported that animal protein had a protective role for bone, especially in elderly women, whereas plant protein was negatively associated with bone mineral density. The hazards of eating a high-protein diet are grossly exaggerated. Certainly, if you have damaged or dysfunctional kidneys, then it would be wise to avoid excess protein.

which protein sources are best?

Let's take a look at what we consider to be several of the best protein sources for athletes.

milk

There's more to milk than making a moustache. In addition to the calcium (which may be a potent fat fighter), an assortment of bioactive peptides or small proteins have been identified in milk. These peptides may improve overall health and well-being. According to the *Journal of*

Dairy Science, "Bioactive peptides [in milk] may function as health care products, providing therapeutic value for either treatment of infection or prevention of disease."

Milk is a complete protein and therefore contains all of the essential amino acids. Generally we'd recommend you consume whole milk if you're the kind of person who skips meals or eats little fat. If you eat clean, however (and follow our advice in chapter 11), than fat-free milk should suffice.

beef

Don't let the fat in beef scare you. In fact, there's a huge difference in fat content between different cuts of beef. For example, ground chuck is 20 percent fat by weight, whereas ground sirloin is only 10 percent fat. A simple method for remembering which beef source has the least fat content is to remember that those at the beginning of the alphabet (ground Chuck) have the most fat and those at the end of the alphabet (ground Sirloin) have the least.

If you remember one thing about beef, it should be ZIP: zinc, iron, and protein. Beef has lots of all three. Also, lean beef is a healthy protein choice. For example, one study published in *Nutrition* looked at overweight women who exercised and consumed a restricted calorie diet with lean beef or chicken as the main protein source. Both groups

---

Nutrients in Top Sirloin Beef

A 6-ounce serving of top sirloin, trimmed of fat and broiled, contains the following nutrients: (326 calories, 51.6 g protein, 11 mg zinc, 5.7 mg iron)

---

lost similar amounts of weight, body fat, total cholesterol, and LDL cholesterol (the bad cholesterol).

chicken

Chicken is a great source of protein. Similar to beef, the fat content of chicken can vary dramatically. Most of the fat in chicken is in the skin. For instance, a 100-gram serving of light-meat chicken with skin contains 222 calories and 10.85 grams of fat, as opposed to 173 calories and 4.51 grams of fat if you remove the skin. That's more than double the fat if you eat the skin. Eating chicken as part of a well-rounded diet can help decrease total cholesterol and LDL cholesterol levels. Although dark meat contains more fat than white meat, try to eat the dark-meat chicken if your overall fat intake is low. This will ensure that you consume the needed fat to keep your cell membranes healthy and your hormone levels normal.

eggs

Some experts consider the amino acid profile of eggs to be the best of all food sources. Eggs are a rich source of thiamine, riboflavin, pan-

Nutrients in Light- and Dark-Meat Chicken Here's how 1 cup of chopped, roasted, skinless dark-meat chicken stacks up nutritionally to 1 cup of white meat.

	CALORIES	PROTEIN	FAT
Dark meat	287	38 g	14 g
White meat	242	43 g	6 g

tothenic acid, folic acid, vitamin B_{12}, biotin, vitamin D, vitamin E, and phosphorus. Although egg yolks have a bad reputation, it isn't entirely deserved. In a study from the *Journal of the American College of Nutrition*, researchers examined 27,000 individuals and found "the daily nutrient intake of egg consumers was significantly greater than that of non-consumers." That is, the egg consumers had a greater daily intake of vitamins B_{12}, C, E, and A. Interestingly, individuals who ate four or more eggs daily had lower blood cholesterol levels than those who ate one egg or fewer a day. Not only is egg protein great, but it's affordable. In a dozen eggs, you get 80-plus grams of protein for less than a dollar!

fish

As we've mentioned many times before, fish is a complete protein that many would rate as the single best protein food source. Why? Eating fish has some amazing benefits. Particularly, the healthy fat in fish (eicosapentanoic acid and docosahexaenoic acid) is something that you won't find in other high-protein foods. There's some evidence that eating fish improves sugar metabolism and decreases your risk of heart disease. Just one serving per week will provide these benefits; however, more frequent consumption is even better.

Macronutrients in an Omelet When you
eat an omelet made from 3 large egg whites and 1 large whole egg, you receive the following nutrients:

206 calories, 23 g protein, 2 g carbohydrate, 11 g fat

---

meal-replacement powders Some-

times you don't have time to fix a real meal. So the best alternative is a protein powder or a meal-replacement powder. Most of these mixes are high in protein, have moderate to no carbohydrates, and have little to no fat. Powders are made from three main sources of protein—whey, casein, and soy. Let's take a closer look at the pros and cons of each.

whey protein

Whey is a complete protein and is particularly high in the branched-chain amino acids (leucine, isoleucine, and valine) and glutamine (an immune-boosting amino acid). Whey is considered a "fast" protein, which means if you eat a serving of whey on an empty stomach, levels of blood amino acids peak about 1 hour afterward and return to baseline within 3 to 4 hours. Thus, whey is an anabolic protein that's great for muscle building or recovery. In fact, you can create an ideal post-exercise meal by combining whey protein with a carbohydrate that's high on the glycemic index, such as maltodextrin, glucose, or sucrose.

casein

Casein is the "opposite" of whey, in that it is a "slow" protein with a lower anabolic effect. Casein stimulates protein synthesis or anabolism by 31 percent versus whey's 68 percent. Casein, however, has a profound anticatabolic effect; meaning that casein inhibits protein breakdown. Because your body digests it slowly, casein produces a slow but steady rise in amino acids. Blood levels of amino acids peak 1 to 2 hours after you eat casein (but they don't get as high as when you eat whey). On the upside, blood amino acid levels stay elevated for up to 7 hours. Casein is a great protein to take before going to bed. Because it's ab-

How the Meal-Replacement Powders Compare Use this chart to gauge the protein content of various meal-replacement powders.

BRAND/PRODUCT	CALORIES	PROTEIN	CARBOHYDRATE	FAT
EAS Myoplex Powder (1 packet)	270	42 g	23 g	3.0 g
GNC Mega MRP (1 packet)	280	40 g	22 g	3.5 g
MET-Rx Original (1 packet)	250	37 g	22 g	2.0 g
Slim-Fast (1 scoop)	100	5 g	20 g	0.5 g

sorbed slowly, you'll get a steady flow of amino acids into your body, which will help your body repair your muscles while you sleep.

soy

Soy is the best nonanimal source of protein. Though most Americans don't consume soybeans on a regular basis, you'll find many palatable soy products (such as soy milk and soy-based protein powders) at your local health food store. Soy protein contains potent antioxidants that provide significant health and anticancer benefits. This may be due to the isoflavones, saponins, phytic acid, and other phytochemicals that soy contains. One recent study found that a diet incorporating a soy-based meal-replacement formula lowered body weight, fat mass, and LDL cholesterol, compared with a diet with the same number of calories but no soy protein.

CHAPTER 13

Fat
why low-fat diets will hurt your running

Let's face it, it's cool to be phat (pretty hot and tempting), not fat. But in your quest to be phat (and, of course, a helluva fast runner), some of you are grossly misinformed into thinking you need to eliminate or severely limit how much dietary fat you eat. Not eating fat, especially the healthy kinds, such as monounsaturated and polyunsaturated fats, can be detrimental to your performance and your waistline.

So what are these healthy fats that you need to eat? Nuts of all kinds, such as cashews, almonds, and peanuts; fatty cold-water fish, such as salmon; and olive oil. If you eat these three foods, which have the right fats, you'll not only be much healthier but also, in the long run (pun intended), a better athlete. Why should you eat healthy fats?

1. "Healthy fats" aren't stored as body fat as easily as the unhealthy fats, such as the animal fats and trans fats.

2. You can eat more fat, still have six-pack abs, and have more energy.

3. These fats are good for your heart!

4. Fats are a good way to consume needed calories when you're training heavily.

5. Besides protein, fats are essential to good health! If you don't eat enough of the essential fats, such as linoleic and linolenic acid (two fats your body cannot manufacture on its own), you'll feel lethargic and unhealthy.

So, as you can see, fat is not the enemy. Underconsume fat and your hair will become brittle, your skin will become dry, and your mood will become . . . well, moody! You need fat for energy, hormone production, cell membrane structure and function, and a host of other valuable things.

three main kinds of fat Let's go over the
different kinds of fats so that you can figure out which fats to limit and which fats to consume. The three main types of fatty acids are saturated, monounsaturated (MUFA), and polyunsaturated (PUFA). A saturated fatty acid has the maximum possible number of hydrogen atoms bonded to every carbon atom. Hence, it is "saturated," or completely filled with hydrogen molecules. On the other hand, a fatty acid with only one double bond is called "monounsaturated" because there are some "missing" hydrogens. Fatty acids having more than one double bond between carbon molecules are polyunsaturated. All foods that contain fat usually contain a combination of these three types of fat in various proportions.

trans and saturated fats

These two fats are a deadly duo. If you enjoy living, I'd suggest you limit your consumption of these fats. Saturated fats are solid at room temperature, so that delicious morsel of fat from that pork chop is probably high in saturated fat. Trans fats (also known as trans fatty acids) are made when food manufacturers turn liquid oils into solid fats. A small amount of trans fat, however, occurs naturally in animal-based foods. Just like saturated fats, trans fats are not your best friend. They can elevate your levels of "bad" cholesterol (LDL), and thus increase your risk of heart disease. Read food labels. If the label says "partially hydrogenated" or "hydrogenated," then that food contains trans fats. You'll find trans fats in foods such as margarines, cookies, snacks, fried foods, and even peanut butter.

Foods That Contain Bad Fats
Cut back on these sources of fat.

- Butter
- Margarine (especially the harder varieties)
- Crackers
- Cookies
- Snack foods
- Baked goods
- Anything made with "partially hydrogenated vegetable oil"
- Certain cuts of beef
- Pork
- Chicken skin
- Whole milk
- Whole-milk cheese

Does this mean that you should eliminate trans fats and saturated fats completely from your diet? No. First of all, it just isn't practical. Secondly, certain foods, such as dairy and meat, contain naturally occurring nutrients that your body needs. For instance, beef is a great source of zinc, iron, and protein. Thus, eliminating beef from your diet isn't the best option. Instead, consume beef once or twice a week (rather than every day) and choose the leanest cuts. In general, opt for the leanest protein sources, such as skinless chicken, or the healthy proteins with fat, such as salmon, most of the time.

the good fats

Researchers have known for many years that high fat intake, at least in the form of olive oil, does not have any apparent negative health effects. Furthermore, we know that monounsaturated fats are less likely to be stored as fat. So keeping that svelte physique is not a problem, assuming

A Brief List of Some Damn Good Fats! Put the following foods back on your menu.

FOOD	% PUFA	% MUFA	% SATURATED
Almonds	17	78	5
Avocado	10	70	20
Canola oil	37	54	7
Cashews	6	70	18
Herring	27	47	26
Macadamia nuts	10	71	12
Olive oil	8	75	16
Peanuts	29	47	18
Salmon	45	38	17
Walnuts	56	28	16

you stick with the good fats. For instance, in an 8-week study done on mice, scientists found that nonexercising mice that were fed beef fat gained more body fat than mice fed a monounsaturated fat diet.

Monounsaturated fats are healthy fats found in nuts, avocados, and oils. Olive and canola oil contain more monounsaturated fats than polyunsaturated fats. Chris Lydon, M.D., author of *Look Hot, Live Long*, says, "Unsaturated fats can help reduce circulating triglyercides and decrease your risk of cardiovascular disease, stroke, obesity, and diabetes!" For example, a 30-week study in which subjects consumed lots of peanuts, which are high in monounsaturated fat, lowered their serum, or blood, levels of fat (specifically triglycerides), and reduced their risk of cardiovascular disease.

Polyunsaturated fatty acids (PUFAs) represent quite a varied number of fats, and some of these polyunsaturated acids are more beneficial than others. The omega-3 fats found in fish (called eicosapentanoic acid [EPA] and docosahexanoic acid [DHA]) are great for you. Yet, many people would rather stick a nail in their thumb than eat fish. Indeed, most Americans consume plenty of linoleic acid (an omega-6 PUFA found in corn, cottonseed, and soybean oils), but usually not enough of linolenic acid (an omega-3 PUFA found in walnuts, flax, and fish). Although it's best to aim for a 1:4 ratio of omega-3s to omega-6s, most people probably eat closer to a 1:20 ratio. In other words, most of us consume 20 times more omega-6s than omega-3s.

somethin' fishy here . . .

Fish is such a great source of fat (and protein) that it deserves special mention. Fish is one of the best foods you can eat, period! The protein is great and the fat has tremendous health benefits. The omega-3 fats found in certain fish (for example, salmon) are something that no athlete should be without. Why are these so important? It's these tongue-twisters: EPA and DHA. Greenland Eskimos who eat lots of fish have a lower incidence of heart disease, arthritis, and psoriasis. Many scientists have attributed this to the large quantities of fish fat they consume. The beneficial effects of fish fat are numerous. For runners, fish fat's anti-inflammatory role may be particularly important. Inflammation is a normal and necessary component of skeletal muscle adaptation to intense exercise. If you increase your consumption of fish, you may be able to speed up your postexercise recovery process. The richest sources of EPA and DHA are cold-water fish, such as salmon, sardines, mackerel, herring, trout, and pilchards. EPA and DHA fatty acids make up 15 to 30 percent of the oil content of these fish.

Another nice benefit of fish is that one of its fats, EPA, helps prevent muscle wasting with certain diseases. This doesn't mean you should wait until you're wasting away before you visit the local fish market. On the contrary, it's just one more example of why fish is a potent health food. According to sports nutritionist, Douglas Kalman, M.S., R.D., of Miami Research Associates, "Fish is the best source of the omega-3 fats, DHA, and EPA; and it would behoove all runners to consume fish regularly."

Health Benefits of Fish Studies show that the two main fats found in fish, EPA and DHA, produce the following benefits.

- Improved blood vessel function in individuals with heart disease
- Reduced risk of death from heart disease
- Less risk of injury to the heart
- Lower blood fat (triglyercide) levels

other types of fat
Usually, when you hear about fat, you only hear about the saturated, trans, and unsaturated varieties. Yet, there is are many other types of fat, several of them beneficial. Let's take a look at some.

Diglycerides. Although we don't often hear about diglycerides, it doesn't mean they are not important. Found in commercially designed supplements, diglycerides are similar to triglycerides. They both have a glycerol molecule as their backbone, but triglycerides have three fatty acids attached to the glycerol (hence "tri"), whereas diglycerides have only two fatty acids attached (hence "di"). In an investigation performed at the Chicago Center for Clinical Research, researchers tested two 24-week diets on overweight men and women. The participants consumed foods that contained either diacylglycerols or triacyglycerols. The diacylglycerol group lost more body weight and body fat. There's obviously something special about this fat. With a growing body of evidence showing the benefits of diacylglycerols, you may be hearing more about them.

Medium chain triglycerides (MCTs). These fats, found in commercially prepared supplements, are a shortened version of the long-chain triglycerides. MCTs are 8 to 10 carbons long, whereas LCTs are 12 to 18 carbons long. In one study, overweight men who consumed more MCTs versus LCTs over a 4-week period lost more weight and were better at oxidizing (burning) fat. For some reason, our bodies are better at burning MCT fat than LCT fat.

Conjugated linoleic acid (CLA). Found in dairy products, CLA was first known as a fat that could help lab rats and mice get lean, very lean. There are some intriguing effects in humans as well. Besides having a dramatic effect on weight loss in mice, CLA may help you regain lean body mass after going off a diet. To test this theory, scientists placed 26 men and 28 women on a very low calorie diet of about 500 calories daily for 3 weeks. After 3 weeks, the participants resumed a normal diet and took either 1.8 grams of CLA, 3.6 grams of CLA, or a placebo daily for 13 weeks. The 500-calorie diet lowered body weight, fat mass, and fat-free mass significantly. That was expected. After the 13 weeks of intervention and going back on a normal diet, however, the CLA groups regained fat-free mass better than the placebo groups. Also, resting metabolic rate was higher in both CLA-supplemented groups than in the placebo group. This of course is due to the increase in fat-free mass, as a pound of muscle burns roughly 35 calories a day just to maintain itself. According to this study, taking 1.8 to 3.6 grams of CLA daily for 13 weeks might help you regain lean body mass. Not too shabby.

Just the Fat Facts To maximize the benefits of fats in your running, follow these pointers.

- Eat fish fat once a week
- Use olive oil–based salad dressing
- Eat nuts as a snack
- Consume roughly 30 percent of your calories from fat
- Limit your intake of saturated and trans fats
- Eat red meat only twice per week; eat whole eggs every other day
- If you are thinking of trying CLA, MCTs, or diacylglycerol supplements, talk to a sports nutritionist first

CHAPTER 14

Carbohydrates
the so-called sacred nutrient

When many runners think of carbohydrates, they think of "carbohydrate loading" or "energy." Some even have visions of their favorite Italian dish overflowing with pasta. Suffice it to say that carbohydrates have definitely received the best press out of the three major macronutrients. Next to fat and protein, most runners view carbs as sacred.

We don't want to be a wet blanket, but, in reality, of the three major macronutrients (proteins, carbohydrates, and fats), carbohydrates are not essential. They are not required in your diet. In contrast, your body cannot manufacture its own fats and proteins, making these macronutrients essential. There are essential fats and essential amino acids (the building blocks of protein), but there is no such thing as an essential carbohydrate or sugar.

Nevertheless, carbohydrates are an important part of the nutrition regimen of runners. There are, however, good carbs and bad carbs. Also, the time when you consume carbohydrates can impact performance and recovery! So how much carbohydrate do you really need? Certainly, the conventional wisdom holds that carbohydrates should make up the majority of one's caloric intake. On that we agree. Exactly how much of a majority, on the other hand, is debatable. One thing we

Which Essential Nutrients Do Humans Need?

In the *American Journal of Clinical Nutrition*, Dr. Eric C. Westman of Duke University Medical Center lists the following essential nutrients.

- Water
- Calories
- Amino acids (histidine, isoleucine, leucine, lysine, methionine, phenylalanine, threonine, tryptophan, and valine)
- Essential fatty acids (linoleic and alpha-linolenic acids)
- Vitamin E
- Vitamin K
- Thiamine
- Riboflavin
- Niacin
- Vitamin B_6
- Pantothenic acid
- Folic acid
- Biotin
- Vitamin B_{12}
- Minerals (calcium, phosphorus, magnesium, and iron)
- Trace minerals (zinc, copper, manganese, iodine, selenium, molybdenum, and chromium)
- Electrolytes (sodium, potassium, and chloride)
- Ultra trace minerals

No carbohydrates make the list.

know for sure: Most runners overconsume carbohydrates and under-consume protein and fat. Another thing we know for sure: 5-K and 10-K runners do not need as much carbohydrates in their diets as ultra-endurance athletes, such as marathon runners and triathletes. In this chapter, we'll provide the information you need to consume the right carbs in the right amounts to best power your running body.

if it's in a box, don't eat it Stay away
from processed carbohydrate foods (and we use the word "foods" loosely here). For example, as much as you might love Oreo cookies, don't buy 'em. If you like white bread, stop right there. If eating your mom's chocolate chip cookies is nothing less than an out-of-body ex-perience, well, okay, have a couple. Our point is this: You need to con-sume (most of the time) carbohydrates that occur naturally in the food chain—that is, carbs that are unprocessed. For example, fruits, vegeta-bles, and beans are wholesome foods that Mother Nature has created for us to eat. On the other hand, crackers are made from the flour that is made from wheat that has most of its redeeming healthful qualities processed out of it. Crackers do not grow on trees or sprout from the earth.

Go ahead and eat as many fruits and vegetables as you like. Maximize whole-grain, minimally processed carbs, such as slow-cooking oatmeal, brown rice, whole-grain bread, and quinoa. Although these carbs have been processed to some extent, they still closely resemble the true oats, rice, and quinoa that grow in nature. On the other hand, their more processed counterparts, such as instant oatmeal and white rice, have had the outer covering of the grain stripped off to speed cooking. The outer covering of the grain contains most of the fiber and good nutrition of a grain. Once you remove it, you're essentially left with empty calories.

As a general rule, minimize your consumption of processed carbs, such as cookies, cakes, crackers, white breads, and white rice. We won't tell you to never eat another Oreo again for the rest of your life. Indeed, Oreos are quite tasty. Just treat your body as a finely tuned machine, and give it the best fuel possible. Don't fill it with low-octane junk food on a regular basis.

what percentage of carbohydrates is ideal? Although most books will tell you that 60 to 75 percent of your total calories should come from carbohydrates, there is no single ideal ratio of carbohydrates to proteins to fats for your diet. Such a ratio would depend on how much total food and calories you consume daily. Rather than thinking of carbs as a percentage of calories, it's better to concentrate on eating enough carbohydrates to fuel your running.

For example, if you're starving yourself on a 500-calorie diet, your carbohydrate intake will be inadequate even if it makes up 70 percent of your total intake. In fact, your fat and protein intake will be too low as well! On the other hand, if you're consuming 3,000 calories per day, then a diet consisting of 40 percent carbohydrates should be more than enough to meet your needs. Keep in mind that you need essential amino acids and fatty acids. Also, amino acids as well as glycerol (from fat) can serve as another source of glucose or glycogen.

Some of you have heard how important carbohydrate consumption is for the runner. Much of these recommendations, however, apply to long-distance competition at the half-marathon or marathon distances. If you're an 800-, 1500-, 3000-, or even 5000-meter runner, you need not worry about running out of glycogen (stored carbohydrate) during a race. You need to run for at least an hour and a half to deplete the stored glycogen in your muscles. If your typical workout and race is less than that, you shouldn't be concerned with carbohydrate loading.

Running a full-length marathon (26.2 miles) requires a different training strategy as well as a different nutritional program than running a 5-K or 10-K. Let's face it, running for 2½ hours at 5 to 7 minutes per mile requires a different approach than doing 60- to 70-second quarters for 1500 meters around a track. In the marathon, you're dealing with dehydration, glycogen depletion, and severe local muscle fatigue. In the 1500-meter event, dehydration and glycogen depletion are *not* factors in the race. Fatigue typically sets in during the last half-lap. That fatigue during the 1500-meter event is primarily the result of a build-up of lactic acid and an inability to tolerate severe pain during the latter portion of the race. It isn't due to glycogen depletion. On the other hand, fatigue during a marathon has nothing to do with lactic acid, but everything to do with glycogen depletion, dehydration, and mental fatigue.

Thus, if you are running shorter distances, focus on eating un-processed carbohydrates. Try to consume a carbohydrate-containing food at each of your six meals. This will ensure a steady stream of energy for you without overdoing it, leaving you enough room in your stomach to eat the protein and fat that your running body needs. To make sure you eat all the macronutrients in the right amounts, each meal you eat should consist of a lean source of protein (such as baked fish); a high-fiber, natural, complex carbohydrate (such as brown rice); a fibrous vegetable (such as salad, broccoli, or cauliflower); and a touch of unsaturated fat (such as olive oil mixed into your salad).

Some of you may be wondering if there's any benefit to carbo-loading—that is, the strategy of some runners of eating as much pasta as they can the night before a big event. Let's say that tomorrow you're running your best event, the 3000 meters. Your time 2 weeks ago was 9:50. You're thinking that you might actually shave a few seconds off this time. Would it help if you went on a carbohydrate binge the day before the meet? Probably not. In fact, it might even hurt your performance. For every gram of muscle glycogen stored, you will also store 2.7 grams of water. This means that you'll weigh more. Athletes often say that after carbo-loading, they feel bloated or heavy. Well, they are. They have gained a pound or two in water weight. For an event like the 3000 meters, a couple extra pounds can make the difference between getting a PR (personal record) and running your worst time ever. More important, how much glycogen you store in muscle is not a limiting factor for performance in distances as far as the 10,000 meters.

So why have you heard so much about carbo-loading? If you look at the scientific studies in this area, you'll find that carbohydrate loading improves performance if the exercise bout lasts 90 minutes or longer. Even then, a recent study showed that carbo-loading had no effect on a 100-kilometer cycling time trial! These cyclists were exercising for 147 to 149 minutes. Regardless, last time we checked, there was no distance in high school or college in which runners (even the slowest ones) took 90 minutes or longer to complete. So, there is no need to carbo-load.

following the glycemic index When

it comes to planning your training meals, your carbohydrate sources should be not only unprocessed but, ideally, also high in fiber and low on the glycemic index (GI). This index is a measure of how quickly your blood sugar rises after you eat a specific type of carbohydrate. Interestingly, simple sugars or carbohydrates do not always have a higher GI than complex carbohydrates. For example, fruit and sweetened dairy products produce a blip in the glucose curve. Table sugar is higher, but amazingly, bread and potatoes rank near the top of the index!

Consuming a diet that's packed to the gills with high-GI foods can prove disastrous to your waistline. By now you know that even though Americans eat less and less fat, they keep getting fatter! What gives? Well, they have, in all likelihood, "replaced" fat consumption with sugar consumption. I'm sure the gain isn't from eating too many apples and oranges. It's probably from eating too many high-GI foods, such as cookies, cakes, and assorted junk food.

In one study, young obese boys who ate a meal composed of high-GI foods tended to eat more later in the day than when they ate a meal composed of lower-GI foods. Researchers also studied the effects of high-, medium-, and low-GI meals eaten during breakfast and lunch. They then measured how much these boys ate for the 5-hour period after lunch. When compared with the low-GI meal, voluntary food intake was 53 percent greater after the medium-GI meal and a whopping 81 percent greater after the high-GI meal. Insulin levels were dramatically higher after the high-GI meal. Even though each meal had the same number of calories, it's clear that the impact on hunger and satiety was different. High insulin levels combined with a tendency to eat more afterward makes it easier for you to gain body weight and fat.

Besides being bad for your waistline, high-GI foods are also bad for your heart. Though having a healthy heart and being disease-free is hardly a concern for most runners, it's still wise to eat as well as you can. Eating high-GI foods can increase your risk of coronary heart disease. In fact, a study in women found that eating high-GI carbohydrates was by itself a good predictor of heart disease, meaning the more you ate, the greater your risk of heart disease.

The biggest reason you should avoid high-GI foods is their effect on your running performance. Consider the following evidence:

- Low-GI foods consumed in the hour before exercise may ameliorate the decline in the blood sugar level that occurs at the start of exercise. In other words, you'll reduce the use of carbs as a fuel and increase the use of fat for energy. If you're going out

---

Fast Track Tip   One way to ensure you stock up on the right foods and minimize the wrong ones is to stick to the outside or perimeter of the grocery store when you shop. This area of the grocery store is where you'll find fruits and veggies, dairy, and meat products, most of them unprocessed. Usually the junk and processed food is shelved in the middle of the grocery store. Avoid these inner aisles. So stay on the outside, and avoid the inside!

---

for a 75-minute training run, consume a small bowl of oatmeal about an hour before.

• Consuming high-GI foods promotes a dramatic rise in the blood sugar level and a corresponding rise in the hormone insulin level, as insulin tries to clear the excess glucose from your bloodstream. Oftentimes, you'll feel hungry soon after eating a high-GI carb. This sequence of events may promote excessive energy intake later in the day, and you'll put on extra pounds as a result. It also might make you feel tired during your workouts.

• Scientists compared the effects of four different meals (ranging from a low- to high-GI rating) on a group of cyclists who were instructed to pedal to exhaustion. The meals included boiled lentils (low-GI rating = 29), baked potato (high-GI rating = 98), sugar (high-GI rating = 100), and water (no GI rating). The blood sugar level dropped dramatically in the potato and sugar

GI Rating of Commonly Consumed Foods Consult this chart to learn the GI rating of various foods.

HIGH GI	MODERATE GI	LOW GI
Glucose	Corn	Apples
Carrots	Sucrose	Navy beans
Honey	Potato chips	Kidney beans
Corn flakes	Peas	Lentils
White bread	White pasta	Sausage
White rice	Oatmeal	Fructose
New potatoes	Oranges	Peanuts
Shredded wheat	Special K cereal	Whole milk
Bagel	Buckwheat	Chocolate
Jelly beans	Brown rice	Low-fat yogurt

groups, right at the start of exercise. The lentil group burned more fat during exercise than the sugar or potato group, and the lentil group lasted longer on the bike test than the other groups.

- In a similar study, women who consumed a moderate-GI food 45 minutes before an exercise test lasted 16 percent longer on a bike test to exhaustion than when they consumed a high-GI food.

Although you could buy a GI index guide and consult it before you eat every single food, such tedium is unnecessary. In our *Fast Track* eating plan in chapter 11, we've already sorted the high-GI foods from the low-GI foods. Just stick with the "Foods You Should Eat Most of the Time" list, and you'll do just fine. An easy rule-of-thumb: Eat natural, unprocessed carbohydrates and as many fruits and vegetables as possible. If it's in a package, don't eat it. Remember, there are no pasta trees, bagel bushes, or bread shrubs. That stuff just isn't natural.

CHAPTER 15

Nutrition Before, During, and After Exercise
eat and drink the right foods and beverages at the right times and your times will improve

If there's just one dietary strategy that all runners should use, it's the following: Consume a beverage that contains carbohydrate and protein immediately after training or competition. Consume at least 20 grams of protein, preferably fast-absorbing protein such as whey, mixed with some healthy, nutrient-filled carbohydrate, such as bananas, mangoes, or your favorite fruit. Put it in a blender, mix it, and drink it as soon as you can after training.

This is the new science of nutrient timing. Scientists have figured out that when you eat or drink is as important as what you put in your body. For instance, research has proven that consuming a carbohydrate-protein supplement immediately after training increases lean body mass more than if you take the same supplement 2 hours after exercise. That's true even if you eat the same total calories throughout the day!

If you forget all the rules of clean eating, if you can't figure out why eating unprocessed carbohydrates is healthier for you than Twinkies, if you would rather die in a flaming plane crash than eat leaner proteins, then at the very least follow the above advice. If you ignore this advice, you'll be missing out on an important and fleeting window of time in which your body craves and most easily absorbs nutrients. If you miss out on this precious window, you won't recover as quickly and you won't run as well during your next workout.

That's just a glimpse of nutrient timing science. There are even more strategies you can use before, during, and after training to maximize performance and recovery. Let's take a look at each.

eating before exercise Research shows
that consuming a carbohydrate-containing supplement before exercise will improve your running performance. In a study from the Georgia Institute of Technology, researchers asked 12 highly trained male distance runners to drink water or a 6- or 8-percent carbohydrate-electrolyte drink before and during a 15-kilometer run. Runners who drank the 6- or 8-percent carbohydrate-electrolyte drink improved their running performance, particularly during the final 1.6 kilometers of the run! Thus, taking the beverage seemed to have a beneficial effect toward the end of the run, when fatigue tends to set in.

Another study led by one of the preeminent sports nutrition scientists, Dr. Rick Kreider, examined carbohydrate use in U.S. National

Field Hockey Team members. Seven members of the team drank carbohydrate solution containing 1 gram per kilogram of body weight of carbohydrate four times daily. Seven other team members ingested a placebo (a sweet-tasting, no-calorie solution) for 7 days of intense training. The group that consumed the carbohydrate supplement had a greater improvement in time to maximum exhaustion and experienced less postpractice psychological fatigue than the placebo group.

Drinking a carbohydrate solution works best for workouts or races lasting longer than 1 hour. You can use this strategy before a long training run or a cross-country race. Another good time to consume a carbohydrate drink is just before doing hard intervals on the track.

eating during exercise You can also consume a carbohydrate solution during exercise, especially if your session will last longer than 1 hour. This strategy is mainly for training runs. Clearly, you can't have someone hand you something to eat or drink in the middle of a 10,000-meter race on the track. If your training runs are long and intense, however, you should consume a carbohydrate-containing beverage during your workout.

In one study, seven well-trained male cyclists exercised at either 45 or 75 percent of their max VO_2. On different days during this workout, they consumed a placebo, a 10-percent liquid carbohydrate supplement, or a solid carbohydrate supplement. They pedaled for 124 minutes, took a rest, pedaled again for 190 minutes, and then rode to exhaustion, working at 80 percent of their max VO_2. When the participants consumed the liquid or solid carbohydrate, they lasted 20 to 30 minutes longer during the pedal to exhaustion than they did when they ingested the placebo beverage. So it may not matter whether you ingest a solid or liquid carbohydrate, but any carbohydrate is definitely better than none. Even though this study was done on cyclists, the same principles apply to runners.

When consuming a drink during exercise, choose one that contains glucose, sucrose, maltodextrin, or all three types of carbohydrate sugars. Fatigue is often delayed by 30 to 60 minutes when you consume these sugars. Stay away from drinks that contain the sugar fructose, because this sugar has been shown to cause gastrointestinal distress.

eating after exercise
Ah, now we're back to where we started, the short window of time after a workout when your muscles are most receptive to absorbing the carbohydrate and protein that you feed them. This, indeed, is one of the most important pieces of dietary advice you can follow. We highly recommend it! Even if you have no appetite, get something in your stomach.

Here's some evidence to back up our convictions. A study from the University of North Texas asked athletes to consume either a carbohydrate-protein solution (53 grams of carbohydrate, 14 grams of protein, 1.5 grams of fat, along with added vitamins, minerals, and amino acids) or Gatorade (21 grams of carbohydrate and no protein or fat) immediately after cycling for 2 hours at moderate intensity. They drank the same solution again 2 hours later. Time to exhaustion during a subsequent workout was 55 percent greater in the athletes who consumed the carbohydrate-protein solution. These athletes also stored 128 percent more muscle glycogen than the Gatorade group.

Protein is an important part of the mix because it helps promote better glycogen storage and, even more important, it aids muscle tissue repair. According to the University of North Texas researchers, "Recovery supplements should be consumed to optimize muscle glycogen synthesis as well as fluid replacement." Other studies have found similar results. For instance, one study found that "postexercise supplementation improved time to exhaustion during a subsequent bout of endurance exercise."

Recovery after exercise is key to a long, healthy running lifestyle. For those of you who are talented enough to make a living at running, it's absolutely critical that you optimize your recovery by consuming some protein and carbohydrate soon after exercise. Even if you're a recreational runner, this tactic will help you feel better during your next run.

After a bout of exercise, you want to do three things:

1. Restore fluids and electrolytes. This is why it's best to consume a beverage rather than whole foods.

2. Replenish muscle glycogen. This is why you need carbs. Your body will most readily convert simple sugars and carbs that are high on the glycemic index into muscle glycogen after your workout.

3. Repair skeletal muscle fibers. This is why you need to consume protein and amino acids.

nutrient quality matters! It not only
matters when you consume nutrients but also which nutrients you con-

sume. We'll go over some of the more important nutrients that should be part of your nutrient timing program.

whey and casein

When you think of protein powders, think whey and casein protein. Whey protein is great for helping muscles repair and rebuild. Additionally, it offers unique health benefits. Casein, on the other hand, is an ideal nighttime protein. Cottage cheese, for example, is full of casein protein. It's a great protein source to take before going to bed because it's slowly digested and absorbed, thus giving your body a slow and sustained release of amino acids into your bloodstream.

Fast Track Tip Between 5 and 10 minutes before exercise or a race, consume a carbohydrate that's high on the glycemic index, such as an energy gel. Experiment with different carbohydrate options during training, however. Everyone's body responds differently to different forms of carbohydrate, and you don't want to suddenly find out on race day that your stomach rebels when you consume one type instead of another. (This applies to all nutritional suggestions, by the way.) Similarly, experiment during your workouts by consuming a sucrose, glucose, or maltodextrin drink (any of the commercially available sports drinks will do). Just avoid fructose. After training or competition, consume about 200 to 500 calories. For example, a carbohydrate-protein drink that contains 40 grams of carbohydrate, 20 grams of protein, and 2 to 3 grams of fat will work fine.

essential amino acids

The building blocks of proteins are amino acids. Recent work has shown that consuming a drink or supplement with essential amino acids plus carbohydrates before exercise results in 160 percent greater net phenylalanine uptake than consuming the same drink postexercise. That translates into a greater potential anabolic effect. For runners, that means your muscles recover better from hard, intense training runs.

The amino acid leucine is particularly great for muscle recovery. For instance, in one study, a leucine-supplemented meal helped restore muscle protein synthesis in old rats. Also, in adult rats, daily supplementation with leucine improved muscle protein synthesis. The researchers speculated that leucine supplementation may be one way to obtain gains in protein without having to necessarily eat a high-protein diet.

antioxidants—vitamin e and c

Vitamin E supplementation may reduce some of the free-radical–induced muscle damage typically inflicted during hard workouts. Endurance athletes appear to benefit particularly well. Supplementation of 800 IU of vitamin E daily induces a 300 percent elevation of alpha-tocopherol (vitamin E) in blood and 53 percent elevation in muscle fibers within about 2 weeks. This is beneficial for type I, or slow-twitch, muscle fibers.

Vitamin C supplementation is effective in reducing the incidence of upper respiratory tract infections after prolonged endurance exercise. Thus, vitamin C is a critical micronutrient that athletes should consume, especially after a hard workout.

CHAPTER 16

Hydration
water versus sports drinks

Which is better, water or a sports drink? That's a tough question to answer. There are situations in which sports drinks are a must, especially during your long training runs, but there are other times when either water or a sports drink will suffice, such as during your shorter workouts (less than 45 minutes).

Nonetheless, remaining well-hydrated is important, particularly if you live in a hot climate, such as Florida, Texas, or Arizona. Then you better be prepared to deal with the heat! If you live in one of these climates, it's probably a good idea to drink copious amounts of water throughout the day, even when you aren't training. If you don't like water, there are several drinks that are basically calorie-free that would be a good substitute. For example, various fitness waters on the market taste great and contain no calories. Let's face it, if given the choice between not drinking water versus drinking one of the big-name brands of flavored water, then that's a no-brainer. Drink the flavored water!

the science of rehydration In one

study, scientists looked at the effect of carbohydrate ingestion before and during exercise. On four separate occasions, they asked seven endurance-trained men to cycle for 2 hours at roughly 63 percent of their peak power output, followed by a time trial. During the four separate workouts, the cyclists drank one of the following solutions:

- A placebo beverage 30 minutes before exercise and every 15 minutes during exercise
- A placebo beverage 30 minutes before exercise and a carbohydrate beverage (2 grams per kilogram; 6.4 percent solution) every 15 minutes during exercise
- A high-carbohydrate beverage (2 grams per kilogram; 25.7 percent carbohydrate solution) 30 minutes before exercise and a placebo beverage every 15 minutes during exercise
- A high-carbohydrate beverage (2 grams per kilogram; 25.7 percent carbohydrate solution) 30 minutes before exercise and a carbohydrate beverage (2 grams per kilogram; 6.4 percent solution) during exercise

What happened? When the cyclists drank a high-carbohydrate beverage before exercise and a carbohydrate beverage during exercise, their time trial performance improved. The researchers concluded that the best way to hydrate and improve performance during exercise is to consume a carbohydrate beverage before and during exercise. Keep in mind that some athletes cannot digest a high carbohydrate solution just before exercise without significant stomach upset, which is why a regular 10% sports drink solution works best.

That's just one study. There are many other studies that show the same thing. Keeping your body hydrated is so important. Your performance will drop if you lose too much fluid and electrolytes. Maintaining fluid balance affects several key areas, including temperature regulation, heart function, and cognitive function. Whenever you exercise (in the heat particularly) and lose fluid, your ability to dissipate heat is compromised. This in turn may compromise your ability to exercise, because you will overheat. Also, cardiac output (the amount of blood your heart pumps in a given time frame) will be diminished because you have more viscous blood to pump. Remember, blood is primarily water. If you lose fluid as a result of exercise, you will impair your cardiac output. Finally, some evidence indicates that moderate levels of dehydration can lead to cognitive impairments.

In general, the amount of fluid your intestines can absorb depends primarily on how much you drink and the calorie content of the drink. Too much sugar may slow digestion during exercise, thus impeding your body from absorbing the fluid and electrolytes from your beverage. That's why some sugar-filled soft drinks may be too concentrated for you to drink during a training run. Some runners take a cola drink (with sugar and caffeine), and let it get flat. They either drink that straight, or they dilute it by one-half and drink it. We suggest, however, that before you try any of these strategies at a race, you test it out during one of your training runs.

Besides improving your performance, staying hydrated may also help you burn body fat. Water accounts for 65 to 75 percent of the weight of muscle. The notion that we should drink eight glasses of water per day makes sense in that our bodies are basically reservoirs of water. Because your body's chemical reactions all occur in a fluid environment, it follows that you need to keep your body well-hydrated so that all of

---

SURPRISING BUT TRUE
COFFEE DOES NOT DEHYDRATE YOU OR IMPAIR YOUR ABILITY TO EXERCISE

If you've heard the notion that drinking coffee or another caffeine-containing beverage will dehydrate you and impair your performance, think again. It isn't true! Here's the proof. A study from Ohio State University compared the effects of caffeinated and noncaffeinated carbohydrate-electrolyte drinks on urine volume during 1 to 4 hours of rest followed by 3 hours of cycling at 60 percent max VO_2. They also tested maximum performance at 85 percent max VO_2 after the 3-hour exercise trials. Throughout the two rest trials and the two rest and exercise trials, participants consumed a carbohydrate-electrolyte beverage, either with or without caffeine. At rest, the average urine volume was greater for caffeine versus placebo. During exercise, however, there was no difference in urine volume between the caffeine and placebo groups. More important, cycling performance was not affected by caffeine. Another study from the Center for Human Nutrition in Omaha, Nebraska, also concluded that consuming caffeine-containing beverages doesn't substantially affect your hydration status.

---

these chemical reactions proceed smoothly and efficiently. So even if you aren't thirsty, try to drink water or a no-calorie, flavored water throughout the day!

glycerol—a better hydrating agent? Glycerol, also called glycerin, is a sweet, syrupy, col-

orless liquid that is used as a sweetener. If you pull out your dust-covered biochemistry books, you'll notice that much of the discussion of glycerol deals with the fact that it's an important component of the triglyceride (fat) molecule. In fact, glycerol forms the backbone of the triglyceride molecule and contains about 4 calories per gram.

Because glycerol helps you retain more fluid, some scientists theorize that consuming glycerol might help performance. This is based on the fact that if you keep yourself well-hydrated, then you'll be able to train harder and longer, particularly in hot environments. In reality, glycerol is probably only beneficial to athletes participating in ultra-endurance sports taking place in hot, humid conditions. This is where the threat of dehydration is the greatest.

A study published in *International Journal of Sports Medicine* showed that glycerol might help exercise performance. In this two-part investigation, researchers set out to determine whether preexercise glycerol ingestion, when compared with preexercise placebo hydration, lowered heart rate, and prolonged endurance time during submaximum-load cycling. They also wanted to learn whether the same preexercise regimen followed by a carbohydrate-replacement solution during exercise would affect the same body responses. Glycerol ingestion lowered average heart rate by 2.8 beats per minute. When a carbohydrate solution was consumed during exercise, glycerol lowered heart rate by 4.4 beats per minute. Glycerol also prolonged endurance time by 21 percent.

There are a few glycerol-containing rehydration beverages on the market; however, some individuals complain of stomach upset and headaches after drinking them. As with any food or supplement regimen, it is always best to try these out during practice first.

CHAPTER 17

Sports Supplements
for Runners
vitamins, minerals, and drinks
that may improve performance

Ergogenic aids are defined as anything that can help you improve performance. Typically, an ergogencic aid refers to performance- enhancing supplements. For instance, consuming carbohydrates that are high on the glycemic index (GI) during a marathon run will improve performance. Hence, in this case, carbohydrates are an ergogenic aid. On the other hand, consuming the same carbohydrates 1 hour before weight training will not improve your performance in the gym. In that particular case, carbohydrates would not be considered an ergogenic aid.

Thus, the use of ergogenic aids is situation-specific. A more broad interpretation of ergogenic aids would include using the best training equipment (such as weights and running shoes), having the best coach, having the best doctors and scientists helping you, and so on. In a sense, all of those are examples of things that can aid performance, making them all ergogenic. For the purposes of this chapter, however, we'll stick to those ergogenic aids that typically fall under the rubric of dietary supplements (with one notable exception that you'll find fascinating).

As an athlete, you might be asked whether you take supplements. For most individuals, the word *supplements* connotes visions of hormones, foul-tasting protein powder, or gobs and gobs of pills with various wacky ingredients. Also, many people think of supplements as products that only bodybuilders take. If you want big muscles, then take supplements, the theory goes.

Nothing could be further from the truth. We'd bet that 100 percent of runners out there are consuming supplements without realizing it. For instance, do you drink calcium-fortified orange juice? Do you eat breakfast cereal fortified with vitamins and minerals? Do you drink a sports beverage before, during, or after training? Do you drink vitamin D–fortified milk? Countless food products are now supplemented with folic acid, among other vitamins and minerals. Now you can even buy vitamin-fortified water! So, as you can see, a supplement doesn't have to come in a pill. It can also come in the form of a particular food or beverage, especially if scientists have altered that food or beverage by adding in vitamins, minerals, herbs, amino acids, and other extras.

supplements as a training tool

We want to make one thing clear. Sports supplements aren't meant to take the place of clean eating. Eating a diet that consists of low-GI carbohydrates, lean proteins, and healthful fats is paramount to your daily nutritional regimen. Think of supplements as the icing on the cake of your eating program.

Supplements are another training tool you can use to enhance performance and recovery, so why not use the best supplements available? Let's take a look at the most important supplements for runners.

carbohydrate-protein supplements

As you learned in chapter 15, it's critical that you consume a carbohydrate-protein combination soon after exercise. Carbohydrates alone will help, but adding protein is even better. In a study published in the *Journal of Strength and Conditioning Research*, researchers compared a carbohydrate-protein beverage (53 grams of carbohydrate, 14 grams of protein, 1.5 grams of fat, along with added vitamins, minerals, and amino acids) to Gatorade (21 grams of carbohydrate and no protein or fat) by conducting a 2-part study looking at endurance performance in cyclists.

In part 1 of the study, they asked cyclists to ride a bike for 2 hours to deplete levels of muscle glycogen. After the 2-hour ride, the cyclists drank either the carbohydrate-protein beverage or the Gatorade. Immediately afterward, they performed a ride to exhaustion at an intensity of 85 percent of their maximum oxygen uptake. The cyclists who consumed the carbohydrate-protein beverage lasted 31 minutes on average; the Gatorade group lasted 20 minutes. The addition of protein to the mix results in 55 percent better endurance.

In part 2 of the study, researchers determined how well muscle energy reserves (that is, muscle glycogen) were restored after exercise. Researchers asked the cyclists to consume either the carbohydrate-protein drink or the Gatorade drink immediately and then again at 2 hours after prolonged exercise. The cyclists who consumed the carbohydrate-protein combination stored 128 percent more muscle glycogen than the cyclists who consumed the Gatorade!

Other studies have shown that as little as 100 calories (roughly equal parts carbs and protein) consumed right after exercise can also promote muscle recovery.

If you're wondering why consuming a protein-carbohydrate mix is better immediately after exercise, it's part of the new science of nutrient timing we discussed in chapter 15. Scientists aren't completely sure why, but they theorize that your muscles are exquisitely sensitive to taking in nutrients after exercise. If you wait 2 hours or longer, your muscles lose some of that sensitivity.

Also, you recover better if you consume carbohydrate and protein in combination, rather than carbohydrate alone. A faster recovery means the next day when you train, you'll feel better and therefore train better or harder. Ultimately, rapid recovery combined with consistent training will produce faster race times.

caffeine

Caffeine—that wonderful stimulant found in coffee, tea, and cola sodas—is probably one of the most effective ergogenic aids that endurance athletes can use. Scientists have found that you can boost your short-term power (such as a 100-meter swim sprint) as well as endurance (such as a 1500-meter run, 1500-meter swim, or cycling race lasting longer than 1 hour). Interestingly, one method that bodybuilders and fitness competitors use to get "cut up" or "ripped" is to drink black coffee or take a caffeine tablet in the morning and then do aerobic exercise.

Caffeine is a mild stimulant of the central nervous system (the brain). Thus, for many individuals, the waking up effect of caffeine can make the perceived effort of exercise much easier. Also, caffeine helps mobilize fat so that you burn more fat and less muscle glycogen during exercise. For longer endurance events lasting an hour or more, this latter adaptation is key, because your body holds an almost endless supply of fat but a limited supply of muscle glycogen.

If you decide to use caffeine, the best dose, according to research, is roughly 5 milligrams of caffeine for every kilogram of body weight, consumed just before exercise. In pounds, that's 2.3 milligrams of caffeine for every pound of body weight. For a 100-pound runner, that equals about 230 milligrams, or 2 to 3 cups, of brewed coffee. Although caffeine is relatively safe for athletes, too much of it can make you nervous, jittery, or anxious. Also, some athletes find it causes gastrointestinal upset.

calcium—a fat-loss mineral?

Calcium isn't an ergogenic aid in the traditional sense; however, it's an important mineral that's lacking in the diets of many young female athletes. Unless you're a regular milk, cheese, or yogurt consumer, you may not be getting enough calcium. A whopping 99 percent of your calcium is stored in your bones. Now surely you know about the importance of calcium for strong bones and teeth. Well, calcium may have another role. It may keep you from getting fat! Yes, calcium may act as a fat-loss mineral.

Research has shown that high-calcium diets increase fat breakdown. If you overeat, a high-calcium diet might prevent some of the weight gain. If you undereat, a high-calcium diet might help preserve your metabolic rate. On the other hand, a low-calcium diet can impair your ability to lose fat. Dairy products like fat-free milk work best, but calcium supplements are also effective. We suggest that you consume at least 1,200 milligrams of calcium a day. A cup of low-fat milk has about 300 milligrams of calcium, and an ounce of Swiss cheese has about 270 milligrams. Vegetables such as broccoli (1 cup = 70 milligrams) and spinach (1 cup = 245 milligrams) are also good sources.

colostrum

Colostrum is a component of breast milk that may aid performance. In one study, researchers fed newborn pigs either pure colostrum formula, normal pig milk, or formula (identical to the colostrum formula without the colostrum). Then they examined muscle biochemistry and metabolism. The colostrum-fed piglets produced the greatest increase in muscle protein synthesis (32 and 39 percent higher in the pig milk and colostrum formula, respectively). Thus, colostrum contains factors that are anabolic (promote muscle mass gains) in skeletal muscle. So there is magic in mother's colostrum.

Okay, that's great for Porky the piglet, but what about humans? Believe it or not, there is quite a bit of scientific data supporting the use of colostrum as a protein-rich sports supplement. For instance, a study done at the University of Nebraska-Kearney found that active men and women who consumed 20 grams daily of bovine (cow) colostrum for 8 weeks increased their lean body mass by about 3.3 pounds. That isn't all. Several studies have shown that bovine colostrum supplementation can increase peak anaerobic power, improve sprint performance, improve time trial performance after a 2-hour bicycle ride, and enhance recovery! Furthermore, contrary to the worries of elite level athletes, colostrum supplementation has no effect on plasma IGF-1 levels, so it won't make you test positive at a competition.

iron

Iron is important because it's a part of the hemoglobin molecule in the red blood cell and is needed in various energy-producing parts of the muscle cell. Some female athletes consume too little iron, particularly if they eat little red meat. In fact, if your levels of hemoglobin (the part of your blood that carries oxygen) and iron are low, you'll develop what's called iron-deficiency anemia. Iron supplements may be warranted in this case. You can also boost iron intake by increasing your consumption of red meat, which is rich in heme iron, a type of iron that is best absorbed by the body. Consuming a vitamin C–rich food or beverage along with an iron-rich food or supplement will also increase absorption of this mineral. If your diet is iron-poor, an iron supplement of 10 to 15 milligrams per day may be needed.

multivitamin/mineral supplements

Although multivitamin/mineral supplements won't help you run faster or longer, there are other compelling reasons to add a multi to your daily supplement regimen. First, look at taking a multi as insurance against poor eating. None of us eats perfectly all the time. Plus, training may increase your need for certain vitamins and minerals. Add those two factors together, and you can easily end up deficient, so it makes sense to take a daily multi. Also, there's strong evidence that taking a multi might decrease the risk of many diseases.

According to an article published in the *Journal of the American Medical Association*, "Suboptimal folic acid levels, along with suboptimal levels of vitamins B_6 and B_{12}, are a risk factor for cardiovascular disease, neural tube defects, and colon and breast cancer; low levels of vitamin D contribute to osteopenia and fractures; and low levels of the antioxidant vitamins (vitamins A, E, and C) may increase risk for several chronic diseases. Most people do not consume an optimal amount of all vitamins by diet alone. Pending strong evidence of effectiveness from randomized trials, it appears prudent for all adults to take vitamin supplements."

In summary, taking a multi provides a lot of benefit with very little risk.

HiLo

You're probably wondering what a HiLo is. Okay, this ergogenic aid does not come in a pill or a food. Rather, it's a technique for improving your race times. Although it's extremely effective, it unfortunately isn't something available to the average runner. You'll see that there's a problem of geography! We'll explain.

HiLo refers to living at high altitude (above 8,000 feet), and training near sea level. So live high, and train low, or HiLo. The theory is based on the fact that your body creates more oxygen-carrying red blood cells at altitude to make up for the lack of oxygen in the atmosphere. This increases your body's ability to carry oxygen and, therefore, deliver it to your exercising muscles. If more oxygen gets to your muscles, then theoretically, your run times will improve. If you also trained at high altitude, however, this may not help much, because the lack of the oxygen in the atmosphere would hinder your workouts. Yet, when you descend to a lower altitude, those extra blood cells will make the air you breathe seem particularly oxygen-rich. You'll have more energy and your performance will improve during your workouts. In short, you'll train better.

In one study, researchers asked college runners to live at an altitude of 8,200 feet and train at a lower level of 4,100 feet. The runners' endurance performance during their training sessions increased by 1.4 percent. In another study, researchers studied 14 elite male runners and 8 elite female runners. The runners lived at high altitude (8,200 feet) for 27 days and trained at a lower altitude (4,100 feet). The runners' sea-level 3,000-meter time trial performance improved by 1.1 percent. To top it off, one-third of the athletes achieved a personal best for the distance. The average men's 3000-meter times before the HiLo was 8:18.4. After living at high altitude, however, their average time dropped to 8:12.6. For the women in the study, their times dropped from an average of 9:32.4 to 9:26.9. Let's face it, at the elite level, these are great improvements! Every second you can shave off your time is a victory in and of itself. Thus, if you have the means, living at altitude for at least 1 month while training at lower altitudes can be helpful to performance. Many athletes have tried to simulate this by using an altitude tent while they sleep. The science on this is still in its infancy; however, it makes sense theoretically that an altitude tent could help your running performance.

So why don't you train at altitude as well? The problem with training at altitude is that you'll sacrifice training intensity and speed. The low partial pressure of oxygen will drastically decrease the quality of your training runs. The best strategy is to live at high altitudes so that your body can adapt with greater oxygen-carrying capacity, and then train at low altitude so that you can train with the needed intensity and speed.

CHAPTER 18

Weight Loss
it's about calories *and* macronutrients!

Weight loss is probably the single most controversial topic in America! Most adult Americans are out-of-shape, overweight couch potatoes, and an entire industry has surfaced to help such people drop the excess pounds. There is a plethora of books on diet and weight loss in bookstores these days, many of them hitting the best-seller list over and over again.

Do such diets work? Well, to some extent, all diets work. That is, as long as you stay on them. Not all diets are, in our opinion, the best for meeting the needs of runners. Should you follow a low-carbohydrate, high-protein diet? What about a low-fat, high-carbohydrate diet? There's no easy answer to such questions, because individual biochemical differences affect how we respond to certain foods. Moreover, weight loss should never be the primary goal of a runner. In a sense, a combination of proper training and clean eating will contribute to the appropriate loss of body weight and body fat. It's much healthier to focus on your training plan and clean-eating plan and let your body find its own ideal weight than it is to aim for an arbitrary number on a scale or an arbitrary percentage of body fat.

Although many runners want to race at their ideal racing weight (that is, the weight and percentage of body fat that will help them run their fastest), we recommend a different approach. Don't worry about dieting down to an extremely low body-fat percentage or body weight. If you're 5 feet 2 inches tall, weighing 105 pounds is feasible. If you're 5 feet 8 inches tall, weighing 105 pounds would probably hurt your performance. Don't compare yourself to other runners. You should only compare yourself to one person, yourself! The bottom line is this: If you run your best at 12 percent body fat, then it makes no sense to get leaner. Finding your ideal performance weight and fat level is tough business. It may take some trial and error over the years, so don't aim for one magical body-fat percentage or weight. Instead, focus on the process—the training and eating.

finding your ideal running weight

If you look at competitive runners, you'll see many with very low body-fat levels. Perhaps only bodybuilders have lower body-fat levels. (However, in their sport, they're judged solely on looks!) Most of these runners have developed these bodies naturally. They didn't starve themselves to get there. You can do the same.

The first step is keeping an eating log. Write down everything you eat and drink. This will help you to stay true to your *Fast Track* eating plan. It will also help you be aware of the foods you eat and when you eat them. Whenever you want to know how you're doing, you can just look at your log. It will tell you the percentage of time you eat clean and the percentage of time you eat junk. It will tell you whether you are eating frequent (four to six meals) small meals or whether you habitually skip meals. Your journal doesn't lie.

Below you'll find some additional pointers for achieving your ideal performance weight.

Recover with food, not with starvation. Too many female runners keep a running tally of the calories they burn as they run. Some of these runners make the huge mistake of skipping their postworkout snack to add to this calorie deficit. This couldn't be more detrimental, not only for your performance but also for your body weight as well. It's very important that you consume a postworkout carbohydrate-protein drink immediately after training. This will speed up the recovery process, allowing you to get in a good workout tomorrow. It also will help keep your metabolism running at a high kick, long after your exercise session. There are good beverages with carbohydrates and protein mixed in. Consume one serving right after training, and count it as one of your four to six daily meals.

Eat regularly. You know what happens when you don't regularly put gas in your car. It runs out of gas! The same is true with your body. Never skip breakfast or any other meal. Stick to an average of six meals per day. This will boost your energy levels, help you recover faster from your workouts, and increase your metabolism. It also will prevent you from developing food cravings and binging on junk food. If you don't have time for a meal, consume a meal-replacement shake.

Nix the processed carbs. As discussed in previous chapters, foods such as pasta, white bread, crackers, and snack chips are no better for you than candy, cookies, or cake. Severely restrict your consumption of processed carbohydrates to once per week. So for weight loss, that's 1 cheat meal out of 35 meals per week. For weight maintenance, you can cheat even more (see chapter 11).

Choose vegetables over fruit. Both fruit and vegetables are loaded with disease-fighting nutrients. Yet most vegetables are naturally low in calories, whereas most fruits are higher in calories because of their high sugar content. Restrict your fruit intake to once per week. You can, on the other hand, eat an unlimited number of vegetables, especially high-fiber vegetables such as broccoli.

Choose lean protein. Protein will slow digestion and help keep blood sugar levels steady, both of which will help you feel satisfied for a longer period after a meal. Choose lean protein sources, such as egg whites, baked fish, canned tuna in water, and skinless baked or broiled chicken breast.

Get plenty of calcium. Calcium aids in fat burning. Drink 4 cups of skim milk daily. If you don't eat dairy products, take a calcium supplement equal to 1,200 milligrams a day. Also, as discussed in chapter 17, it's a good idea to take a multivitamin/mineral supplement.

a sample day of eating for fat/weight loss
To see how these tips translate into a day of real eating, consult the menu below. We designed it for a 20-year-old female runner who's 5 feet 2 inches tall and 120 pounds. She runs 35 miles a week and has 19 percent body fat. This menu is de-

signed to help such a runner drop 10 pounds and lower her body-fat percentage. As you can see, the menu contains no processed carbohydrates, high-sugar fruits, fruit juice, or fatty meats, and few calorie-containing beverages.

Meal 1: 3 egg whites mixed with ½ cup of dry oatmeal (mix well; makes oatmeal pancakes); sprinkle on sucralose (Splenda) to make it sweet; drink ½ cup of skim milk

Meal 2: High-protein meal-replacement shake (for example, MET-Rx) (160 calories: 1 gram fat, 2 grams carbohydrate, 35 grams protein)

Meal 3: 1 grilled skinless chicken breast with 1 cup of steamed broccoli; drink 16 ounces of water.

Meal 4 (postworkout): 1 serving of a carbohydrate-protein drink mix (240 calories: 2 grams fat, 37 grams carbohydrate, 17 grams protein); drink 16 ounces of water.

Meal 5: 6 ounces grilled fish, ½ sweet potato, salad with tomatoes and spinach (touch of vinegar and olive oil dressing); drink 16 ounces of water.

Meal 6: ¼ cup of peanuts

Calories: 1440; Protein: 146 grams; Carbohydrate 97 grams; Fat 52 grams

the healthful way to lose weight

If you haven't already noticed, eating to lose fat is not much different from eating for performance. You'll want to stick primarily to lean protein, unprocessed carbohydrates, and healthy fat, in that order. In round numbers, that amounts to roughly 40 percent protein and about 30 percent each of fat and carbohydrates.

At the same time, there's no need to obsess over the percentages of protein, carbohydrates, and fat. Eating should never be about mathematics. Instead, focus on making good food choices. You can't get fat by eating unlimited amounts of grilled fish and broccoli. It's that simple. On the other hand, you certainly can gain fat if you splurge on bread and butter.

Granted, a reduction in total caloric intake will eventually (in most cases) lead to a decrease in body weight. However, what's the nature of that weight loss? Is it mostly fat or muscle? Guess what, the nature of the weight loss is different when you eat high-carbohydrate versus low-carbohydrate diets. In essence, you'll lose more body weight and fat with a low-carbohydrate, high-protein diet. On the other hand, you'll lose more lean body mass on the low-fat diet, high-carbohydrate diet. To top it off, you may be surprised to learn that the low-carbohydrate, high-protein diet is also healthier for you. You lose more weight and more fat and keep more lean body mass—and it's healthier for you.

Here's some recent evidence to support these claims.

low-carbohydrate diets and body composition

Going back to 1994, you can find lots of good evidence that shows a better kind of weight loss on a low-carbohydrate diet. In one such study, scientists put 25 overweight women on two different 800-calorie diets (an amount of calories, by the way, that is much too low for runners). One diet consisted of 45 percent protein, 35 percent carbohydrate, and 20 percent fat; the other consisted of 60 percent carbohydrate, 20 percent protein, and 20 percent fat. After 21 days, both groups lost similar amounts of weight and body fat, but—and this is very important—the high-carbohydrate group lost more lean tissue, most of which was probably muscle. So eating proportionately more protein will in essence spare your muscle.

In 1999, scientists from Denmark did a 6-month study comparing two diets: a high-carbohydrate one (58 percent carbohydrate, 12 percent protein, 30 percent fat) and a high-protein one (45 percent carbohydrate, 25 percent protein, 30 percent fat). They tested the diets on 65 healthy, overweight, and obese participants. Participants in the high-carbohydrate group lost 11.2 pounds (9.5 pounds of fat), whereas those in the high-protein group lost 19.6 pounds (16.7 pounds of fat). In short, the high-protein group lost 75 percent more weight and 76 per-

High-Carbohydrate versus High-Protein Diets As you can see from these results from a study published in the *Journal of Nutrition*, high-protein diets result in more weight and fat loss than high-carbohydrate diets.

TYPE OF DIET	WEIGHT LOSS	FAT LOSS	REDUCTION IN LEAN BODY MASS
High-Protein	16.6 pounds (8.5 percent more than the high-carb group)	5.6 pounds (19.1 percent more than the high-carb group)	1.9 pounds
High-Carbohydrate	15.3 pounds	4.7 pounds	2.7 pounds (42 percent more than the high-protein group)

cent more fat than the high-carbohydrate group. Another interesting aspect of this study was that 35 percent of the subjects in the high-protein group lost more than 22 pounds, compared with only 9 percent in the carbohydrate group.

In 2003, the *Journal of Nutrition* published another article comparing high- versus low-carbohydrate diets. In this study, the high-protein, low-carbohydrate group also lost more weight and more fat, and kept more lean body mass (such as muscle) than the high-carbohydrate group.

For yet another study, led by one of the best researchers in the field of low-carbohydrate diets, Dr. Jeff Volek of the University of Connecticut, researchers asked 12 healthy men to switch from their normal diet (48 percent carbohydrate) to a very low carbohydrate diet (less than 10 percent carbohydrate) for 6 weeks. The results were amazing. Once they switched to a low-carb diet, the men lost 7.5 pounds of fat and gained 2.4 pounds of lean body mass. What's interesting about this study is that the subjects didn't change their activity levels or total caloric intake.

By now it should be clear that merely decreasing caloric intake is only part of the weight-loss story. Sure, you'll lose weight on a restricted calorie, high-carbohydrate diet, but you'll lose it from all the wrong places. Think about it. You're losing more lean body mass on these high-carbohydrate diets—lean body mass that you need to power your running and your metabolism. Although weight loss is almost always associated with a loss of fat and lean tissue, it's better to restrict the carbohydrates and preferentially consume protein. This will have what scientists call a "protein-sparing effect." Essentially, that means you won't lose the precious lean tissue that you need.

how low should you go? Another question that often arises is whether restricted carbohydrate diets are harmful to your health. You've probably heard the notion that eating "too much protein" is bad for your kidneys. Well, let's put that old wives' tale to bed. There's no scientific evidence that eating double, triple, or even quadruple the Recommended Dietary Allowance for protein is harmful for healthy individuals. Why this myth persists is a mystery.

What about heart health? Won't low-carb diets raise your risk of heart disease? Again, the evidence doesn't support this notion. In general, when you compare the typical high-carbohydrate diet to a low-carbohydrate diet, you'll see levels of blood fats, such as triglycerides, decrease; levels of blood sugar improve; and levels of blood

SURPRISING BUT TRUE
THE BENEFITS OF LOW-CARB DIETS OUTWEIGH THE RISKS

According to an elegant review written by Drs. Jeff S. Volek and Eric C. Westman and published in the journal *Diabetes Care*, the benefits of low-carb diets over high-carb diets are as follows:

- Low-carb diets result in greater weight loss than standard diets.
- Low-carb diets tend to suppress appetite more, increase metabolic rate, and make your body more efficient (so you burn more calories).
- Low-carb diets tend to spare lean body mass better than high-carb diets (meaning you'll lose less muscle).
- Low-carb diets have favorable effects on cardiovascular disease risk factors (for example, decreased blood triglyceride levels, increased HDL levels, changes in LDL particle size, and so on).

insulin normalize. In fact, replacing carbohydrates with either monounsaturated fats or lean protein sources is clearly a healthier alternative.

In one study published in the journal *Diabetes Care*, scientists compared a high-protein diet (28 percent protein, 42 percent carbohydrate, 28 percent fat) with a high-carbohydrate diet (16 percent protein, 55 percent carbohydrate, 26 percent fat). They split 54 overweight men and women into two groups, with one group on the high-protein diet and the other on the high-carbohydrate diet. Women on the high-protein diet lost more total fat (11.7 pounds versus 6.2 pounds) and abdominal fat (2.9 pounds versus 1.5 pounds) than women on the high-carbohydrate diet. Interestingly, in men, weight loss was similar for the high-protein and high-carbohydrate groups. From a health

SURPRISING BUT TRUE
CALCIUM BURNS FAT

Calcium consumption has been shown to help you burn fat. In a study from the University of Colorado Health Sciences Center, researchers found that the intake of calcium promoted fat burning.

We recommend that you consume 2 to 3 servings of skim milk daily. If you don't normally consume dairy foods, it'll be difficult for you to get enough calcium. Milk, sardines in oil, cheese, yogurt, and broccoli are excellent sources of calcium. If you don't eat enough of these foods, there are many calcium supplements on the market that'll do just fine. Your dietary calcium goal should be 1,200 milligrams a day. There's just no excuse not to get enough of this precious fat-burning mineral!

standpoint, the high-protein group had a greater reduction in LDL (or "bad") cholesterol levels.

If you're confused about the best way to lose weight, you aren't alone. Although high-protein, low-carb diets work best on average, some runners will do just fine on a standard high-carb diet. As a starting point, emphasize lean proteins, unprocessed carbohydrates (such as plenty of vegetables and some fruits), and unsaturated fats. If you make the correct food choices 90 percent of the time, then you'll find that weight loss—or to be more exact, fat loss—will come naturally. As we've mentioned, weight or fat loss should never be a runner's primary goal. Performance is always the main goal. If you perform best at 12 percent body fat, then there's no need to get leaner. Trial and error will eventually bring you to your ideal body weight and body fat for competitive running.

PART 5

Training for Success

CHAPTER 19

Beyond Running
how weight lifting, cycling, and other activities can improve your performance

You're probably wondering whether it's worth your time to head to the gym and lift weights. Will cross-training make you faster? Would it help if once or twice a month you substituted a hard bicycle ride for a long run? Or would swimming be just as effective? And what about stretching—can it really prevent injury? You'll be surprised to learn the answers to all these questions. Let's first address the issue of lifting weights.

lifting weights When you look at the winners of almost any road race, one thing is obvious—these guys and girls are *skinny*. In general, distance runners have slight builds. But it makes sense. To carry your body a given distance, whether it's 1 mile or 26.2 miles, you need to have a low body weight, preferably little fat, and just the right amount of muscle to propel your body.

If you were to take an NFL running back and line him up against an average female cross-country runner in a 1-mile race, it would be no contest. The running back would be eating the female runner's dust in no time. Big muscles don't help in this type of situation.

Okay, so having large, bulbous muscles may not improve your endurance performance, and, as the above example illustrates, it may even detract from it. On the other hand, building strong, toned muscles in the weight room with the right exercises *can* boost your running performance. The difference lies in how you train your muscles. For running, you want strong, toned muscles, not larger muscles. You don't want to be built like a running back, but you do want to be strong enough to propel yourself forward in a race. Weight lifting will definitely help. As a runner, you just need to do it properly. Strengthening your muscles for running requires a different type of weight-training program than the NFL running back, who wants both strong and large muscles.

the iron game

When it comes to the benefits of weight training (a.k.a. strength or resistance training) for endurance, scientific research says it best. Evidence indicates that it improves both short- and long-term endurance capacity and may even improve lactate threshold. For instance, a study from the University of Maryland's Department of Kinesiology found that 12 weeks of weight training improved performance. In this study,

18 healthy but untrained men were randomly assigned to a weight-training or control group. Even though maximum oxygen uptake did not change, cycling time to exhaustion increased by 33 percent. However, this study was done using untrained males. What would have happened if trained athletes were used?

The Department of Physical Education at the University of Illinois at Chicago tested the effects of adding weight training to eight cycling- and running-trained subjects who were already "at a steady-state level of performance." Participants performed weight training three times a week for 10 weeks, keeping their endurance exercises, such as cycling or running, constant. Participants performed the following weight-training exercises:

- Parallel squats (5 sets of 5 repetitions each)
- Knee extensions (3 sets of 5 repetitions each)
- Knee flexions (3 sets of 5 repetitions each)
- Toe raises (3 sets of 25 repetitions each)

Resistance was set at 80 percent of their 1-repetition maximum strength. (A 1-repetition maximum refers to the maximum amount of weight you can lift once.) After 10 weeks of training, leg strength increased 30 percent, but muscle size didn't change, which is good news for runners. Although max VO_2 remained the same, short-term endurance improved by 11 percent and 13 percent, respectively, during a cycling and running session. Long-term cycling to exhaustion improved 20 percent; however, run-time results in the 10-K were inconclusive.

What's the take-home message from this study? First, weight training will not result in big, bodybuilder muscles. If you're doing a significant amount of running or cycling, it will be very, very difficult for you to put on a lot of muscle. Your individual physiology and daily calorie demands won't allow for it. Second, weight training does appear to improve endurance. So, should you lift weights? Definitely. Weight training will help you become a better runner. Remember, however, that it's only one part of the training puzzle. It's much more important to get in your time on the track or the road than your time in the weight room. Rather than hit the weights five times a week, aim for one or two times a week.

plyometrics can make you faster

So, now you understand that regular weight training can improve muscular endurance. But it doesn't always translate into faster race times. This is where plyometric training comes in. Plyometrics (also known as explosive resistance exercises) include skipping, jumping, and an exaggerated running technique called bounding. According to a study from Finland, plyometric training can help you run a faster 5-K distance! Eight elite male cross-country runners (with less than 10 percent body fat) were chosen for the study. (Even though women weren't part of the study, it would make sense that the results could apply to women as well.) On average, they all trained 8 to 9 hours per week, eight to nine times per week. Researchers divided the group in half. In one group, researchers replaced about one-third of their training hours with plyometrics. The other group continued with their usual routine. In addition to running, the plyometric group performed the following exercises:

- Sprints (20 to 100 meters in length)
- Various types of jumps (with and without weights)
- Low-weight leg-press, leg-extension, and leg-curl exercises performed at a high speed

After 9 weeks of training, the plyometric group decreased its 5-K time by roughly 30 seconds, whereas the nonplyometric group didn't improve its 5-K time at all. This study shows that muscle power is an important factor in running performance. By improving muscle power, you can improve running economy (meaning, you can run faster using the same amount of energy). This doesn't, however, mean you need the power of a sprinter.

Interestingly, the plyometric group had no change in max VO_2, yet the control group did. So, as we said in chapter 10, even an increase in max VO_2 doesn't necessarily mean you become a faster runner. Plyometric training, on the other hand, definitely may help your performance by enhancing your running economy. Because plyometrics are an intense form of training, before attempting them make sure you get how-to instructions from a certified weight-training coach first.

Fast Track Tip According to a study from the University of Otago in New Zealand, one bout of high-intensity heavy resistance exercises decreased running economy for up to 8 hours. This means that if you lift weights immediately before you run, your performance could be worse. It's best that you reserve weight training for after your run, not before.

the bottom line on weight training

What is the bottom line on weight training? The previous studies show that weight training does have a proper role in a runner's regimen. With this in mind, we'd recommend that you gradually incorporate weight training and plyometrics into your running program. Work with your weight-training coach to determine if plyometrics once or twice per week can fit into your overall training scheme. As an adjunct to running, weight training (traditional or plyometric) is a great tool to improve your performance.

cross-training helps
Cross-training can be good for you, but it should never replace the bread and butter of your training, which is quality running. Why should you cross-train? There are many reasons, but two of the most important include:

1. To give your joints a break from the pounding of running;
2. To give yourself a mental break from the tedium of running.

For example, if you're running five to six times per week during your off-season, make two of those workouts either cycling, swimming, rowing, or elliptical training. All of these exercises are great low-impact options that will not only rev up your heart rate but also give your leg muscles and bones a chance to recover. Other types of cross-training exercises include upper-body cycling, stairclimbing, rollerblading, and aquarunning (see below).

water training
(also called aquarunning)

Water training is a popular cross-training choice because it decreases the pounding your joints take from running. It can also be used to keep your aerobic fitness at high levels.

During water training, you wear a buoyant vest that keeps you from sinking. Then you run in place in the deep end of the pool, trying to simulate the same form as running on land. One study from Florida State University looked at the effects of a 6-week aquarunning program on aerobic fitness, blood variables, and body composition. Researchers had one group run and the other group do only water training. Both groups responded equally to both types of training, leading the authors to conclude that aquarunning may serve as an effective training alternative to land-based running for the maintenance of aerobic performance.

stretching Interestingly, there is no hard data to show that
regular stretching reduces the incidence of injuries. However, it's our opinion that regular stretching, particularly after exercise, is a great way to maintain good range of motion around your joints. This may improve your running economy and subsequently help your performance. Before you stretch, it may be wise to consult with your weight-training coach.

the big picture By now you should understand that
traditional weight training, plyometrics, aquarunning, and cross-

training are all valuable tools for improving your running performance. Use weight lifting to strengthen your core muscles and improve the strength of muscles around your hips and knee joints. Use plyometrics to help improve your race times, and use aquarunning and other forms of cross-training to give your body a break from the daily grind.

Remember: All of these things (and you can throw in diet and supplements) are training tools. In isolation, none of these tools will be the magical ingredient to running success. However, in combination, when used properly, these tools can make you a better and healthier runner.

CHAPTER 20

Workouts and Training Plans
sample training programs
for the high school, college,
and adult recreational runner

Every goal-oriented runner should have a systematic approach to training. A runner without a plan is like a doctor performing surgery without first going to medical school.

Before you can devise a plan, however, you need some guidance. We know that many of you, whether you are age 15 or 45, often are ill-advised when it comes to training. Worry no more. We're going to make sure this doesn't happen to you. In this chapter, we'll outline fundamental training plans that you can tweak to meet your own needs. Remember, each of us has a unique adaptive response to training.

The training plans in this chapter will serve as a reference for all runners, ranging from high school and college distance runners who compete in the 1500 to 5000 meters, to cross-country runners, to road racers. Before we get started, however, you must first figure out the best plan for you. Follow these steps.

Develop a specific year-to-year plan. We can't provide you with magical workouts or a set number of miles a week that will guarantee success. You must experiment and find the right mix for your individual body and goals. We have, however, included basic principles and guidelines for you to follow that will increase your chances of success.

Determine long-term and short-term goals. To train successfully, you must first determine long-term and short-term goals for a specific season or seasons. For many high school athletes, the long-term goal is performing well at the state meet. In college, the goal may be placing well at a conference or at a regional or national championship. If you're an adult recreational runner, you may have your sights set on a particular race in which you hope to run a personal best or beat your best friend. Once you have determined what your goals are, you can start preparing your body for success.

Implement a training plan. Your training plan should help you to achieve your peak performance level at the right time. It doesn't help you much if your chosen race falls in the middle of the base phase of your plan. Ideally, you want to peak for your race, which means you need enough time to train for it! Our training plans all last 12 weeks, so assuming you start your plan tomorrow, you will peak 12 weeks later. We've broken each plan into specific training phases: base phase, conditioning phase, competition phase, and recovery phase. Below, you'll find a description of the importance of each phase.

base phase

The base phase prepares your body for what comes next. Every distance program starts with base mileage. This is vital because you need to have a strong base of mileage runs to sustain you through a long, intense year of training. You should generally increase your mileage at a rate of 5 to 10 percent a week to be safe.

conditioning phase

During the conditioning phase, you're conditioning your body to perform at a higher level. Here, you will start adding speed or track workouts to your routine one to two times a week, conditioning your body to maintain a faster pace.

competition phase

During the competition phase, your mileage will decrease as you get closer to your goal race. At the same time, your workouts will become more intense. You will also taper your training during this phase by cutting back on mileage before a big race. This gives your body and brain just enough time to recuperate for the big race, but not so much time that you lose your fitness.

recovery phase

During this phase, you'll give your body the TLC it needs to recover from your training. Don't skip this important phase. Too often, runners go from competition phase to competition phase without a break, leading to burnout, overtraining, and injuries. For some runners, recovery means complete rest for 1 to 2 weeks. For others, it entails cross-training or easy running. If you don't incorporate some sort of recovery phase into your training regimen, you significantly increase your chances of injury and mental burnout. It is essential that you allow your body to recover from the intense training phases to ensure longevity.

the *fast track* workouts Once you've

broken your year into these different phases of training (see "Mapping Out Your Training Phases" below), it's time to look at the specific workouts you'll be completing during these various phases. All of these workouts should be done after a 10- to 15-minute warmup and finished with a 10- to 15-minute cooldown.

Mapping Out Your Training Phases

Start your training program at a time of year that allows you to peak for your goal race or races. Below, you'll find examples of how to do this for different race goals.

CROSS-COUNTRY TRAINING

Base Phase: June and July
Conditioning Phase: August and September
Competition Phase: October and November
Recovery Phase: Early December

TRACK TRAINING

Base Phase: Late December and January
Conditioning Phase: February and March
Competition Phase: April and May
Recovery Phase: Early June

---

downhill running

Downhill training will improve your leg turnover; however, because it is very intense, it's probably best that you do this only after you've built a good base. Perform your downhill running on a gradual decline. Allow the hill to gently increase your running speed and turnover. If you're breaking your stride or finding yourself bracing or putting on the breaks, the hill is too steep. Warning: Downhill running can take quite a toll on your quads. Ease into this type of training gradually, and don't do it more than once or twice a week.

fartlek

Fartlek is Swedish for "speed play." Fartlek is an excellent way to build speed without it being too intense. Some coaches incorporate this late in the base phase, whereas others prefer that their athletes build a good base first and then do fartlek training during the conditioning phase. With fartlek, you want to cover 3 to 6 total miles while incorporating surges of various lengths and speeds into your workout. For example, if you run on a trail that includes a lot of telephone poles, you might speed up your pace from one pole to the next, recover to the next pole, and then speed up again. Do this over varied terrain.

hill repeats

As you enter the conditioning phase, hill repeats are a great way to improve leg strength. This is ideal for cross-country running, particularly during the conditioning phase. Hill repeats are similar to interval training. You'll use the uphill for the intense part of your workout and the downhill for recovery. As a start, you may want to find a hill that will allow you to do 60-second repeats. If you live in a state as flat as

Florida, that might be tough. If that's the case, you may need to find stadium steps at your local university.

intervals

Intervals are repeated speed surges of 200 meters or longer followed by a recovery interval. These are great for improving speed and lactate threshold. It's best to do intervals during the conditioning and competition phases. The length of the run and the length of the recovery interval are determined by the phase of training you're in at the time. Some examples of interval workouts would be ten 400-meter intervals with 90-second recovery, or three 1600-meter intervals with 3-minute recovery.

speed endurance

Great for improving performance, speed-endurance training works best during the conditioning and competition phases. During this workout, you'll run at race pace or faster for 200 to 1600 meters, taking a full recovery after each repeat. An example would be three 600-meter runs with 8- to 10-minute recovery.

speedwork

Speedwork improves your maximum running speed, which is critical at the end of the race when you want to outkick your competitors. You'll perform this type of training mainly during the later stages of the conditioning phase and in the competition phase. In this workout, you'll run short, intense sprints of 5 to 150 meters, taking a full recovery after the repeats. An example would be three 50-meter sprints with 3-minute recovery.

tempo running

Tempo running is an excellent way to build endurance. Not as intense as traditional interval or speedwork, tempo training is a great training tool during the base and conditioning phases. Tempo running consists of running at a pace 10 to 30 seconds per mile slower than your current 10-K race pace for a distance of 2 to 4 miles. Tempo runs can be run for time or for a set number of miles.

tempo intervals

Another method for improving speed, tempo intervals are great to do during the conditioning phase. This is a variation of tempo running where you run 400-meter to 2-mile repeats with a short recovery of 30 to 120 seconds. The total distance run in your tempo interval session should equal 2 to 4 miles.

cross-training

Cross-training is an alternative type of exercise, such as aquarunning, biking, elliptical training, or cross-country skiing. Cross-training adds variety and additional work to your training schedule while minimizing the risk of injury. It can also serve as a great substitute for running when you are injured.

form drills

You'll do these to improve your leg turnover. The more efficient your stride, the faster you'll be able to run. I recommend doing form drills after your distance runs. Generally, your form will start to fall apart when you get tired, so it's best to practice good form when you are fatigued after a long run. Some basic drills are:

High knees. Run bringing your knees up to a 90-degree angle.

Buttkicks. Run as if you were trying to kick yourself in the butt with your heels.

Skipping. Just as you did as a young child, you'll skip by exaggerating the height and then the distance of your skips.

Grape vines. Run sideways while crossing one leg in front of the other and then behind.

Backward running. This forces you to concentrate on picking up your feet.

Do each drill for about 50 meters at a time, completing two sets of each.

strides

Strides are 75- to 100-meter short sprints where you start at a moderate pace and gradually build up to a sprint by the end. Do some strides when warming up for a workout or a race. I recommend incorporating strides into your training schedule on the day before a race.

weight, or strength, training

Weight training is an important part of training for a distance runner. The goal, however, isn't to put on mass but, rather, to stay toned. You should concentrate on core strength and upper-body exercises. I recommend incorporating weight training into your workout schedule after your hard workouts on Mondays and Wednesdays. Following this schedule allows you to recover on Tuesdays and Thursdays.

Below, you'll find an example of a 2-day per week weight-training regimen.

Day 1

Wide-grip lat pulldowns: 3 sets of 12 repetitions

Flat bench press: 3 sets of 12 repetitions

Military press with dumbbells: 3 sets of 12 repetitions

Situps: 25 repetitions

Crunches: 25 repetitions

Abdominal-crunch machine: 25 repetitions

Leg lifts: 25 repetitions

Back hyperextensions: 3 sets of 25 repetitions

Leg press: 3 sets of 12 repetitions

Day 2

Narrow-grip lat pulldowns: 3 sets of 12 repetitions

Incline dumbbell bench press: 3 sets of 12 repetitions

Upright rows: 3 sets of 12 repetitions

Situps: 25 repetitions

Crunches: 25 repetitions

Abdominal-crunch machine: 25 repetitions

Leg lifts: 25 repetitions

Back hyperextensions: 3 sets of 25 repetitions

Smith-machine lunges: 3 sets of 12 repetitions

plyometrics

Plyometrics are very difficult exercises that should be incorporated into your training only after you've developed a good base of endurance training. We recommend you consult with your track coach as well as your weight-training coach to see how many times per week you should do plyometrics. We suggest no more than once or twice per week.

sample training program for cross-country runners Below you'll find sample workouts and training plans for each of the three basic training phases involved in 5-K cross-country racing—base, conditioning, and competition. We'll first start with the base phase.

base phase

During the base phase, you want to safely build up your mileage. Start with running 5 days a week for 30 to 40 minutes at a time, and gradually increase your mileage by adding 1 longer day of running each week. As a suggestion, you might start your long runs at 50 to 60 minutes and try to increase that to 75 to 90 minutes at the peak of your mileage. You can also incorporate "two-a-days" into your program (running twice a day). Just be sure that your second run is shorter and generally less intense than your main distance run. Try to get up to 6 days a week of running as you progress. There are many people who like to run every day, which is fine. Just be sure you allow yourself adequate recovery somewhere in the week. At the very minimum, it's a good idea to take a day off every 21 days.

Also, be careful when increasing volume and intensity at the same time. Be sure to listen to your body and adjust your training accordingly. As mentioned earlier, this is just an example. You can make many variations to this program by adding two-a-days and adjusting the mileage to fit your specific needs. But the basic principles still apply: Do not increase your mileage by more than 5 to 10 percent a week, and always include adequate rest days between workouts.

Week 1

Monday: 40-minute run

Tuesday: 45-minute run

Wednesday: 40-minute run

Thursday: 45-minute run

Friday: 40-minute run

Saturday: 60-minute run

Sunday: off or easy running day

Week 2

Monday: 40-minute run

Tuesday: 25-minute run in the morning and 45-minute run in the afternoon

Wednesday: 45-minute run

Thursday: 45-minute run

Friday: 40-minute run

Saturday: 60-minute run

Sunday: off or easy running day

Week 3

Monday: 15-minute warmup; 15 minutes of tempo running; 15-minute cooldown

Tuesday: 30-minute run in the morning and 45-minute run in the afternoon

Wednesday: 50-minute run

Thursday: 20-minute run in the morning and 45-minute run in the afternoon

Friday: 40-minute run

Saturday: 65-minute run

Sunday: off or easy running day

Week 4

Monday: 15-minute warmup; two 10-minute tempo runs with 1-minute recovery; 15-minute cooldown

Tuesday: 30-minute run in the morning and 45-minute run in the afternoon

Wednesday: 15-minute warmup; 10 hill repeats; 15-minute cooldown

Thursday: 30-minute run in the morning and 45-minute run in the afternoon

Friday: 45-minute run

Saturday: 70-minute run

Sunday: off

The Sunday Solution Should you do an "easy" run or take the day off on Sundays? For many runners, the mere thought of taking a day off brings anxiety and distress. We suggest that, in the long run, it's likely better that you take the day off. Giving your body a full day to recover will help you avoid musculoskeletal problems and give you a mental break. Remember: Resting is just as important as exercising and eating.

conditioning phase

During the conditioning phase you want to get your body ready to race. You should maintain your mileage and add more speedwork or track workouts to your training schedule.

Week 5

Monday: 15-minute warmup; three to four 1600-meter intervals with 3-minute recovery; 15-minute cooldown

Tuesday: 30-minute run in the morning and 45-minute run in the afternoon

Wednesday: 15-minute warmup; six 2-minute tempo runs with 30- to 60-second recovery jogs; 15-minute cooldown

Thursday: 30-minute run in the morning and 45-minute run in the afternoon

Friday: 40-minute run

Saturday: 70-minute run

Sunday: off or easy running day

Week 6

Monday: 15-minute warmup; two 10-minute tempo runs with 1-minute recovery; 15-minute cooldown

Tuesday: 30-minute run in the morning and 45-minute run in the afternoon

Wednesday: 15-minute warmup; 10 hill repeats; 15-minute cooldown

Thursday: 30-minute run in the morning and 45-minute run in the afternoon

Friday: 45-minute run

Saturday: 70-minute run

Sunday: off

Week 7

Monday: 15-minute warmup; 1000-, 2000-, 2000-, and 1000-meter intervals with 2-minute recovery; 15-minute cooldown

Tuesday: 30-minute run in the morning and 45-minute run in the afternoon

Wednesday: 15-minute warmup; 2-mile tempo run; 15-minute cooldown

Thursday: 30-minute run in the morning and 45-minute run in the afternoon

Friday: 40-minute run

Saturday: 75-minute run

Sunday: off or easy running day

Week 8

Monday: 15-minute warmup; five to six 800-meter intervals with 90- to 120-second recovery; 15-minute cooldown

Tuesday: 30-minute run in the morning and 45-minute run in the afternoon

Wednesday: 15-minute warmup; three 5-minute tempo runs with 1-minute recovery jog; 15-minute cooldown

Thursday: 30-minute run in the morning and 45-minute run in the afternoon

Friday: 40-minute run

Saturday: 75-minute run

Sunday: off or easy running day

competition phase

Your mileage should start to decrease as your racing intensifies. To peak or reach maximum performance at your goal race, you should taper.

Tapering is a reduction of volume and intensity before an event.

In general, as your fitness increases so does your fatigue. So when training is reduced, your fatigue decreases rapidly. You can maintain your fitness on 50 percent of your previous volume for 3 to 6 weeks. We recommend that you begin your taper 3 weeks out from the goal race. Here is a tapering breakdown:

3 weeks out: decrease volume to 75 percent

2 weeks out: decrease volume to 50 percent

1 week out: you should be at 25 percent of your previous volume.

So, if you average 60 miles a week during the season, you should drop down to 40 miles 3 weeks out, 30 miles 2 weeks out, and 15 miles 1 week out.

Week 9

Monday:15-minute warmup; five 1000-meter intervals with 2- to 3-minute recovery; 15-minute cooldown

Tuesday: 30-minute run in the morning and 45-minute run in the afternoon

Wednesday: 15-minute warmup; fifteen 1-minute tempo runs with 1-minute recovery jog; 15-minute cooldown

Thursday: 45-minute run or cross-training

Friday: 30-minute run

Saturday: 5-K cross-country race

Sunday: 70-minute run

Week 10

Monday: 15-minute warmup; three 1600-meter intervals with 3-minute recovery; 15-minute cooldown

Tuesday: 30-minute run in the morning and 45-minute run in the afternoon

Wednesday: 15-minute warmup; two 3-, 2-, and 1-minute tempo runs with 1-minute recovery jog; 15-minute cooldown

Thursday: 45-minute run or cross-training

Friday: 30-minute run

Saturday: 5-K cross-country race

Sunday: 65-minute run

Week 11

Monday: 15-minute warmup; four 800-meter intervals with 2-minute recovery; six 400-meter intervals with 60-second recovery; 15-minute cooldown

Tuesday: 45-minute run

Wednesday: 15-minute warmup; three 5-minute tempo runs with 1-minute recovery jog; 15-minute cooldown

Thursday: 45-minute run or cross-training

Friday: 30-minute run

Saturday: 5-K cross-country race

Sunday: off or easy running day

Week 12

Monday: 15-minute warmup; three 1000-meter intervals with 2-minute recovery; 15-minute cooldown

Tuesday: 45-minute run

Wednesday: 15-minute warmup; fifteen 1-minute tempo runs with 1-minute recovery jog; 15-minute cooldown

Thursday: 45-minute run

Friday: 40-minute run

Saturday: 5-K cross-country race

Sunday: off or easy running day

sample training program for 1500-meter runners

Below you'll find sample workouts and training plans for each of the three basic training phases involved in racing the 1500 meters.

base phase

Base phase for the 1500-meter runner is the same as for the cross-country runner. Use this time to safely increase your mileage. Start with 30 to 40 minutes a day and build up to 6 days a week. It's also important to include a longer run of 50 to 90 minutes each weekend.

Week 1

Monday: 40-minute run

Tuesday: 45-minute run

Wednesday: 40-minute run

Thursday: 45-minute run

Friday: 40-minute run

Saturday: 60-minute run

Sunday: off or easy running day

Week 2

Monday: 40-minute run

Tuesday: 25-minute run in the morning and 45-minute run in the afternoon

Wednesday: 45-minute run

Thursday: 45-minute run

Friday: 40-minute run

Saturday: 60-minute run

Sunday: off or easy running day

Week 3

Monday: 15-minute warmup; 15-minute tempo run; 15-minute cooldown

Tuesday: 30-minute run in the morning and 45-minute run in the afternoon

Wednesday: 50-minute run

Thursday: 20-minute run in the morning and 45-minute run in the afternoon

Friday: 40-minute run

Saturday: 65-minute run

Sunday: off or easy running day

Week 4

Monday: 15-minute warmup; two 10-minute tempo runs with 1-minute recovery; 15-minute cooldown

Tuesday: 30-minute run in the morning and 45-minute run in the afternoon

Wednesday: 15-minute warmup; 10 hill repeats; 15-minute cooldown

Thursday: 30-minute run in the morning and 45-minute run in the afternoon

Friday: 45-minute run

Saturday: 70-minute run

Sunday: off

conditioning phase

During conditioning phase, you want to get your body ready to race. You should maintain your mileage and add more speed workouts to your training schedule.

Week 5

Monday: 15-minute warmup; three 5-minute tempo runs with 1-minute recovery; 15-minute cooldown

Tuesday: 30-minute run in the morning and 45-minute run in the afternoon

Wednesday: 15-minute warmup; ten 200-meter intervals with 75-second recovery; 15-minute cooldown

Thursday: 30-minute run in the morning and 45-minute run in the afternoon

Friday: 40-minute run

Saturday: 70-minute run

Sunday: off or easy running day

Week 6

Monday: 15-minute warmup; twelve 400-meter intervals with 90-second recovery; 15-minute cooldown

Tuesday: 30-minute run in the morning and 45-minute run in the afternoon

Wednesday: 15-minute warmup; three 150-meter intervals with walk-back recovery and 5-minute recovery between sets; 15-minute cooldown

Thursday: 30-minute run in the morning and 45-minute run in the afternoon

Friday: 45-minute run

Saturday: 70-minute run

Sunday: off

Week 7

Monday: 15-minute warmup; nine 300-meter intervals with 100-meter recovery jog; 15-minute cooldown

Tuesday: 30-minute run in the morning and 45-minute run in the afternoon

Wednesday: 15-minute warmup; nine 200-meter intervals with 75-second recovery; 15-minute cooldown

Thursday: 30-minute run in the morning and 45-minute run in the afternoon

Friday: 40-minute run

Saturday: 65-minute run

Sunday: off or easy running day

Week 8

Monday: 15-minute warmup; four to five 800-meter intervals with 90- to 120-second recovery; 15-minute cooldown

Tuesday: 30-minute run in the morning and 45-minute run in the afternoon

Wednesday: 15-minute warmup; three 150-meter intervals with walk-back recovery and 5-minute recovery between sets; 15-minute cooldown

Thursday: 30-minute run in the morning and 45-minute run in the afternoon

Friday: 40-minute run

Saturday: 60-minute run

Sunday: off or easy running day

competition phase

During the competition phase, you'll be decreasing your mileage and sharpening your speed skills as you look toward your goal races.

Week 9

Monday: 15-minute warmup; five 400-meter intervals with 5-minute recovery; 15-minute cooldown

Tuesday: 30-minute run in the morning and 45-minute run in the afternoon

Wednesday: 15-minute warmup; six 200-meter intervals with 75-second recovery; 15-minute cooldown

Thursday: 45-minute run or cross-training

Friday: 30-minute run

Saturday: 1500-meter race

Sunday: 60-minute run

Week 10

Monday: 15-minute warmup; four 600-meter intervals with 8- to 10-minute recovery; 15-minute cooldown

Tuesday: 30-minute run in the morning and 45-minute run in the afternoon

Wednesday: 15-minute warmup; two 150-meter intervals, two 100-meter intervals, and two 50-meter intervals, with walk-back recovery and 5-minute recovery between sets; 15-minute cooldown

Thursday: 45-minute run or cross-training

Friday: 30-minute run

Saturday: 800- or 3000-meter race

Sunday: 60-minute run

Week 11

Monday: 15-minute warmup; four 400-meter intervals with 10-minute recovery; 15-minute cooldown

Tuesday: 45-minute run

Wednesday: 15-minute warmup; five 200-meter intervals with 75-second recovery; 15-minute cooldown

Thursday: 45-minute run or cross-training

Friday: 30-minute run

Saturday: 1500-meter race

Sunday: off or easy running day

Week 12

Monday: 15-minute warmup; 500-, 300-, and 150-meter intervals with 8-minute recovery; 15-minute cooldown

Tuesday: 45-minute run

Wednesday: 15-minute warmup; two 150-meter intervals, two 100-meter intervals, and two 50-meter intervals, with walk-back recovery and 5-minute recovery between sets; 15-minute cooldown

Thursday: 40-minute run or cross-training

Friday: 30-minute run

Saturday: 1500-meter race

Sunday: off or easy running day

sample training program for 3000- and 5000-meter runners

In general, women who run the 3000 and 5000 meters should gain a comfortable base mileage first. I recommend that high school girls run 25 to 50 miles a week and college females 45 to 75 miles a week. This is a wide range, but everyone is unique. The goal is to run the least amount of miles while getting the maximum benefit. This plan will minimize your risk of injury and allow for steady progression throughout your running career. As runners we have a tendency to always think more is better, and that isn't always the case.

base phase

Base phase is basically the same as cross-country base phase.

Week 1

Monday: 40-minute run

Tuesday: 45-minute run

Wednesday: 40-minute run

Thursday: 45-minute run

Friday: 40-minute run

Saturday: 60-minute run

Sunday: off or easy running day

Week 2

Monday: 40-minute run

Tuesday: 25-minute run in the morning and 45-minute run in the afternoon

Wednesday: 45-minute run

Thursday: 45-minute run

Friday: 40-minute run

Saturday: 60-minute run

Sunday: off or easy running day

Week 3

Monday: 15-minute warmup; 15-minute tempo run; 15-minute cooldown

Tuesday: 30-minute run in the morning and 45-minute run in the afternoon

Wednesday: 50-minute run

Thursday: 20-minute run in the morning and 45-minute run in the afternoon

Friday: 40-minute run

Saturday: 65-minute run

Sunday: off or easy running day

Week 4

Monday: 15-minute warmup; two 10-minute tempo runs with 1-minute recovery jog; 15-minute cooldown

Tuesday: 30-minute run in the morning and 45-minute run in the afternoon

Wednesday: 15-minute warmup; 10 hill repeats; 15-minute cooldown

Thursday: 30-minute run in the morning and 45-minute run in the afternoon

Friday: 45-minute run

Saturday: 70-minute run

Sunday: off

conditioning phase

During conditioning phase you want to get your body ready to race. You should maintain your mileage and add more speed workouts to your training schedule.

Week 5

Monday: 15-minute warmup; five 1000-meter intervals with 3-minute recovery; 15-minute cooldown

Tuesday: 30-minute run in the morning and 45-minute run in the afternoon

Wednesday: 15-minute warmup; two 3-, 2-, and 1-minute tempo

runs with 1-minute recovery jog; 15-minute cooldown

Thursday: 30-minute run in the morning and 45-minute run in the afternoon

Friday: 40-minute run

Saturday: 70-minute run

Sunday: off or easy running day

Week 6

Monday: 15-minute warmup; three 1600-meter intervals with 3-minute recovery; 15-minute cooldown

Tuesday: 30-minute run in the morning and 45-minute run in the afternoon

Wednesday: 15-minute warmup; twelve 200-meter intervals with 200-meter recovery jog; 15-minute cooldown

Thursday: 30-minute run in the morning and 45-minute run in the afternoon

Friday: 45-minute run

Saturday: 65-minute run

Sunday: off

Week 7

Monday: 15-minute warmup; six to eight 800-meter intervals with 400-meter recovery jog; 15-minute cooldown

Tuesday: 30-minute run in the morning and 45-minute run in the afternoon

Wednesday: 15-minute warmup; ten 1-minute tempo runs with 1-minute recovery jog; 15-minute cooldown

Thursday: 30-minute run in the morning and 45-minute run in the afternoon

Friday: 40-minute run

Saturday: 75-minute run

Sunday: off or easy running day

Week 8

Monday: 15-minute warmup; 800-, 1600-, 400-, and 400-meter intervals, with 400-meter recovery jog; 15-minute cooldown

Tuesday: 30-minute run in the morning and 45-minute run in the afternoon

Wednesday: 15-minute warmup; nine 300-meter intervals with 100-meter recovery jog; 15-minute cooldown

Thursday: 30-minute run in the morning and 45-minute run in the afternoon

Friday: 40-minute run

Saturday: 75-minute run

Sunday: off or easy running day

competition phase

During the competition phase, you'll be decreasing your mileage and sharpening your speed skills as you look toward your goal races.

Week 9

Monday: 15-minute warmup; twelve to fifteen 200-meter intervals with 200-meter recovery jog; 15-minute cooldown

Tuesday: 30-minute run in the morning and 45-minute run in the afternoon

Wednesday: 15-minute warmup; three 6-minute tempo runs with 1-minute recovery jog; 15-minute cooldown

Thursday: 45-minute run or cross-training

Friday: 30-minute run

Saturday: 5-K track race

Sunday: 70-minute run

Week 10

Monday: 15-minute warmup; eight 600-meter intervals with 2-minute recovery; 15-minute cooldown

Tuesday: 30-minute run in the morning and 45-minute run in the afternoon

Wednesday: 15-minute warmup; three 5-minute tempo runs with 1-minute recovery jog; 15-minute cooldown

Thursday: 45-minute run or cross-training

Friday: 30-minute run

Saturday: 3-K track race

Sunday: 65-minute run

Week 11

Monday: 15-minute warmup; ten 400-meter intervals with 60- to 90-second recovery; 15-minute cooldown

Tuesday: 45-minute run

Wednesday: 15-minute warmup; nine 200-meter intervals with 200-meter recovery jog; 15-minute cooldown

Thursday: 45-minute run or cross-training

Friday: 30-minute run

Saturday: 5-K track race

Sunday: off or easy running day

Week 12

Monday: 15-minute warmup; 800-, 1600-, 400-, and 400-meter intervals, with 400-meter recovery jog; 15-minute cooldown

Tuesday: 45-minute run

Wednesday: 15-minute warmup; two 3-, 2-, and 1-minute tempo
runs with same recovery; 15-minute cooldown

Thursday: 45-minute run

Friday: 30-minute run

Saturday: 3-K track race

Sunday: off or easy running day

post-college—training for the local 5-k or 10-k road race After a

successful and rewarding high school and college track or cross-country
running "career," your goals will probably change (unless you're a
world-class runner). If your goal is to run a local 5-K or 10-K road race,
clearly, you may not have the luxury to train as hard and as often as you
did during college. However, you can still obtain and maintain excellent cardiovascular conditioning and remain competitive at the local
level.

How should you train if you're no longer in college and have a husband, two kids, one dog, a pet hamster, and a mortgage to pay? Well,
clearly your life's priorities have shifted; however, the same basic principles of training used by high school and college runners apply here.
There's one major caveat. Most of you don't train to peak for a certain
track meet or cross-country event. In fact, most of you like running that
local 5-K race hoping to best your time of the previous week. If you
don't run any faster, it's no big deal.

For the average recreational runner, the programs listed in this
chapter are too intense. First of all, most runners don't have the time

to train that much, and secondly, your body just cannot take the pounding it used to and recover as quickly. However, if you're still in tip-top shape and can finish in the top five of a local 5-K road race, then feel free to follow the programs listed here. Otherwise, just keep the following pointers in mind.

- Keep running fun.
- The day after a race, take a day off.
- Once a week, do a long distance run of about 10 miles at a conversational pace.
- Once a week, do speedwork, such as running up stadium steps or a 100-yard hill with a gradual incline 10 times and walking down.
- After you run, consume a protein-carbohydrate shake.
- If you have any nagging lower-extremity joint pain, stop running and do nonimpact cardiovascular exercises.
- On hot days, make sure you hydrate yourself with a sports drink.
- Every 4 months, take at least one week off completely from running.
- Always warm up before running.
- Always cool down after running.

For more information on running programs for recreational runners, go to Road Runners Club of America at www.rrca.org.

The training programs in *Fast Track* were designed by Division I cross-country and track coach Cami Wells, of Bowling Green University.

Glossary

Aerobic: This refers to the production of energy in the presence of oxygen. The aerobic breakdown of carbohydrate and fat provides most of the energy during endurance exercise.

Altitude tent: A tent that pumps in a regulated amount of oxygen to simulate living at altitude.

Amenorrhea: A lack of menstrual periods in a postpubescent woman.

Amino acids: A group of nitrogen-containing, carbon-based organic compounds that serve as the building blocks from which protein (and muscle) are made.

Anaerobic: This refers to the production of energy without oxygen. Sprinting and weight lifting use energy mainly from anaerobic sources.

Anaerobic energy pathway: This energy system provides energy for exercise that is intense and short-term in nature (less than 60 seconds).

Anemia: A deficiency of iron in the blood. If you don't consume enough iron (found in foods such as red meat and beans), your body may run low on hemoglobin (the protein in red blood cells that carries oxygen to the tissues). If your tissues become starved of oxygen, you will become weak and tired.

Anorexia (also called anorexia nervosa): An eating disorder where an individual overly restricts calories in order to say thin.

ATP (adenosine triphosphate): This high-energy molecule is stored in muscle and other cells in the body. When a muscle cell needs energy, ATP is broken down to provide this energy. ATP can be thought of as the actual fuel that makes muscles move.

Bonking: Crashing or getting extremely tired during a race or workout due to insufficient fuel in the body.

Bounding: A form of plyometric training where exaggerated knee lifts and strides are emphasized to strengthen muscles and improve flexibility.

Bulimia: An eating disorder where an individual binge eats and then vomits in order to lose weight.

Carbohydrates: These are organic compounds containing carbon, hydrogen, and oxygen. Carbs are the primary fuel source for the body during intense exercise. The different types of carbohydrates include starches, sugars, and fibers, and are classified into three groups: monosaccharides, disaccharides, and polysaccharides. Carbohydrates contain 4 calories per gram. Glucose (blood sugar) is a carbohydrate used by every cell in the body as fuel.

Cross-training: Supplementing other sports along with your running. Some options include swimming, aquarunning, biking, rowing, inline skating, walking. Cross-training helps save your running muscles from the daily pounding of running. It also strengthens different muscle groups than running, and can help prevent injuries.

Diagonals: A running exercise where you stride diagonally across a soccer field, then jog the baselines.

Downhill running: Downhill running should be done on a very gradual decline. The idea is to work on improving leg turnover. If you are breaking your stride while running the downhill, the hill is too steep.

Eccentric loading: During weight lifting or plyometrics, the eccentric portion of a muscle contraction occurs during the lengthening phase of contraction. For example, during a biceps curl, your muscle strengthens eccentrically as you lower the weight and extend your arm, and your biceps muscle lengthens.

800s or **800 meters:** These are equivalent to a half-mile, or two laps around a standard track.

Electrolytes: Substances such as sodium that are capable of conducting electricity. These charged particles are present throughout the body and are involved in activities such as regulating the distribution of water inside and outside of cells.

Ergogenic: Possessing the ability to enhance work output, particularly as it relates to athletic performance.

Fartlek: Swedish word for "speed play." With fartlek, you want to cover 3 to 6 total miles while incorporating surges of various lengths and speeds into your workout. Do this over varied terrain.

Fat-free mass (FFM): All portions of body tissues not containing fat, such as bones, muscles, skin, organs, water, hair, blood, and lymph.

400s or **400 meters:** These are equivalent to a quarter-mile, or one lap around a standard track.

Free radicals: Highly reactive atoms or compounds having an unpaired electron. Free radicals are produced during metabolism and are believed to cause cellular damage. They may play a rule in aging and disease.

Fructose: The main type of sugar found in fruit. Sweeter than table sugar, fructose is often used as a sugar substitute for diabetics.

Glucosamine: A supplement that is said to regenerate joint cartilage and reduce the progression of osteoarthritis.

Glucose: This is the simplest sugar molecule. It's also the main sugar found in blood, and it is used as a basic fuel for the body. Too much blood glucose will cause your body to release a rapid and large amount of insulin.

Glycemic index: A ranking of carbohydrates based on their immediate effect on blood glucose (blood sugar) levels. It compares foods' carbohydrate contents, gram for gram. Carbohydrates that break down quickly during digestion have the highest glycemic indexes, causing the blood glucose response to be fast and high. Carbohydrates that break down slowly, releasing glucose gradually into the bloodstream, have low glycemic indexes.

Glycogen: The principal stored form of carbohydrate in muscle and liver.

HDL: High-density lipoprotein, one of the subcategories of cholesterol. It is typically thought of as the "good" cholesterol.

Hill repeats: Similar to interval training, these use the uphill for the intense part of your workout and the downhill for recovery.

Hormones: Hormones regulate various biological processes through their ability to activate or deactivate enzymes.

Hypertrophy: An increase in muscle size.

Hypoglycemia: An abnormally low amount of sugar in the blood.

Insulin: An anabolic hormone secreted by the pancreas that aids the body in maintaining proper blood sugar levels and promoting glycogen storage. Insulin secretion speeds the movement of nutrients through the bloodstream and into muscle for growth.

Intervals: Repeated distances of 200 meters or farther followed by recovery intervals. The length of the run and the length of the recovery interval are determined by the phase of training you are in at the time. Some examples of interval workouts would be 10 times 400 meters with 90-second recovery, or 3 times 1600 meters with 3-minute recovery.

Lactic acid: This molecule is produced from glucose during anaerobic metabolism. When oxygen become available, lactic acid can be completely broken down into carbon dioxide and water. Lactic-acid buildup is a primary cause of muscle fatigue.

LDL: Low-density lipoprotein, a subcategory of cholesterol that is typically thought of as the "bad" cholesterol.

Lean body mass (LBM): Another term that describes fat-free mass.

Low-glycemic foods: Foods with a low-glycemic index raise blood sugar levels slowly after eating and can help prolong physical endurance.

Meal-replacement powders (MRPs): This category of supplements contains protein, carbohydrates, vitamins, minerals, and other key nutrients which are used to replace a regular-food meal for purposes of weight loss, weight gain, or increasing dietary nutrient intake.

Metabolic rate: This refers to the rate at which your body converts energy stores into working energy in the body. In other words, it's how fast your "whole system" runs. The metabolic rate is controlled by a number of factors, including muscle mass (the greater your muscle mass, the greater your metabolic rate), caloric intake, exercise, and use of stimulant or depressant chemicals.

Metabolism: The sum total of all anabolic and catabolic reactions in the body.

Organic: Pertaining to agricultural products that are grown using biological, mechanical, and cultural methods as opposed to synthetic methods to control pests, enhance soil quality, or improve processing.

Osteoporosis: The loss of bone mineral density and the inadequate formation of bone.

Overtraining: Training so much that your performance is compromised.

Oxidation: The process by which oxygen is added to a compound and/or electrons are lost. Oxidation is involved in the derivation of energy from compounds and causes the release of free radicals.

Plyometrics: Bounding exercises; any jumping exercise in which landing is followed by another jump.

Proteins: These highly complex nitrogen-containing compounds are found in all animal and vegetable tissues. They are made up of amino acids and are essential for growth and repair in the body. A gram of protein contains 4 calories. Those from animal sources are high in biological value since they contain essential amino acids. Those from vegetable sources contain some but not all of the essential amino acids. Proteins are broken up by the body to produce amino acids that are used to build new proteins. Proteins are the building blocks of muscle, enzymes, and some hormones.

Rabbit: A fast runner who sets a fast pace for other runners in a race but doesn't finish. His/her main goal is to get the runners to push the pace early on.

Running economy: The amount of oxygen you use when you run. When you improve your economy, you are able to run at a given pace while utilizing less oxygen.

Saturated fats: "Bad" fats that have been shown to raise cholesterol levels in the body. They are called saturated because they contain no open spots on their carbon skeletons. Saturated fats include myristic acid, palmitic acid, stearic acid, arachidic acid, and lignoceric acid. Sources of these fats include animal foods and hydrogenated vegetable oils, such as margarine.

Sucrose: Most commonly known as table sugar, this is derived from sugar cane or sugar beets. When you eat sucrose, your body breaks it into fructose and glucose.

Tapering: Cutting back on your training/mileage before a big race

Tempo intervals: This is a variation of tempo running where you run 400-meters to 2-mile repeats with short recoveries of 30 seconds to 2 minutes. The total distance run in your tempo interval session should equal 2 to 4 miles.

Tempo runs: Runs of 20 to 30 minutes in length at 10- to 15-seconds-per-mile slower than 10-K race pace. An example of a 20-minute tempo run might be a 10-minute warmup, a 20-minute run at tempo pace, and a 10-minute cooldown. Another way to gauge the pace of tempo runs: a pace about midway between short-interval training speed and your easy running pace.

Unsaturated fats: "Good" fats that have been shown to help reduce cholesterol and triglyceride levels in the blood. They are called unsaturated because they have one or more open carbon spots.

Unsaturated fats can be divided into two categories: polyunsaturated fasts and monounsaturated fats. This category of fats includes the essential fatty acids linolenic and linoleic acids.

Vitamins: These organic compounds are vital to life, indispensable to bodily function, and needed in minute amounts. They are noncaloric essential nutrients. Many of them function as coenzymes, supporting a multitude of biological functions.

VO_2 max (maximal oxygen consumption): The maximal amount of oxygen that a person can extract from the atmosphere and then transport and use in the body's tissues.

Selected Bibliography

Chapter 5

Zemel, M. B. "Role of Dietary Calcium and Dairy Products in Modulating Adiposity," *Lipids* vol. 38 (2003): 139–46.

Chapter 6

Bilz, S., et al. "Effects of Hypoosmolality on Whole-Body Lipolysis in Man," *Metabolism* vol. 48, no. 4 (1999): 472–76.

Chapter 7

Bass, M., L. Turner, and S. Hunt. "Counseling Female Athletes: Application of the Stages of Change Model to Avoid Disordered Eating, Amenorrhea, and Osteoporosis," *Psychol Rep* vol. 88 (3 Pt. 2) (June 2001): 1153–60.

Beals, K. A., and M. M. Manore. "Disorders of the Female Athlete Triad among Collegiate Athletes," *International Journal of Sport Nutrition and Exercise Metabolism* vol. 12, no. 3 (Sept. 2002): 281–93.

"The Female Athlete Triad: A responsible approach for coaches," *USOC/ACSM Consensus Statement* (2002).

Golden, N. H. "A Review of the Female Athlete Triad (Amenorrhea, Osteoporosis and Disordered Eating)," *International Journal of Adolescent Medicine and Health* vol. 14, no. 1 (Jan.–Mar. 2002): 9–17.

Hobart, J. A., D. R. Smucker. "The Female Athlete Triad," *American Family Physician* vol. 61, no. 11 (June 1, 2000): 3357–64, 3367.

Hobart, Julie A., M.D., and Douglas R. Smucker, M.D., M.P.H. *The Female Athlete Triad* (American Academy of Family Physicians, 2000).

Kazis K., and E. Iglesias. "The Female Athlete Triad," *Adolescent Medicine* vol. 14, no. 1 (Feb. 2003): 87–95.

Kleposki, R. W. "The Female Athlete Triad: A Terrible Trio of Implications for Primary Care," *Journal of the American Academy of Nurse Practitioners* vol. 14, no. 1 (Jan. 2002): 26–31.

Leonard, N. H., L. L. Beauvais, and R. W. Scholl. "Work Motivation: The Incorporation of Self-Based Processes, *Human Relations* vol. 52 (1999): 969–98.

Loud, K. J., M.D., and L. J. Micheli, M.D. "Common Athletic Injuries in Adolescent Girls," *Current Opinion in Pediatrics 2001*, vol. 13: 317–22.

Montero, A., S. Lopez-Varela, E. Nova, and A. Marcos. "The Implication of the Binomial Nutrition-Immunity on Sportswomen's Health," *European Journal of Clinical Nutrition* vol. 56, suppl. 3 (Aug. 2002): S38–41.

Otis, C. L. "Too Slim, Amenorrheic, Fracture-Prone: The Female Athlete Triad," *ACSM's Health and Fitness Journal* vol. 2, no. 1 (1998): 20–25.

Sabatini, S. "The Female Athlete Triad," *American Journal of Medicial Science* vol. 322, no. 4 (Oct. 2001): 193–5.

Chapter 9

Brooks, G. A. "Current Concepts in Lactate Exchange," *Medicine and Science in Sports and Exercise* vol. 8 (Aug. 1991): 895–906.

McArdle, W. D., F. I. Katch, and V. I. Katch. *Exercise Physiology 4th edition* (Baltimore: Williams & Wilkins, 1996), 130

Chapter 10

Bassett, D. R., and E. T. Howley. "Limiting Factors for Maximum Oxygen Uptake and Determinants of Endurance Performance," *Medicine and Science in Sports and Exercise* vol. 32 (2000): 70–84.

Grant, S., et al. "The Relationship between 3-Km Running Performance and Selected Physiological Variables," *Journal of Sports Science* vol. 15 (1997): 403–10.

Jones, A. M. "A Five-Year Physiological Case Study of an Olympic Runner," *British Journal of Sports Medicine* vol. 32 (1998): 39–43.

Trappe, S. W., et al. "Aging among Elite Distance Runners: A 22-Year Longitudinal Study," *Journal of Applied Physiology* vol. 80 (1996): 285–90.

Yoshida, T., et al. "Physiological Characteristics Related to Endurance Running Performance in Female Distance Runners," *Journal of Sports Science* vol. 11 (1993): 57–62.

Yoshida, T., et al. "Significance of Contribution of Aerobic and Anaerobic Components to Several Distance Running Performances in Female Athletes, *European Journal of Applied Physiology* vol. 60 (1990): 249–53.

Chapter 11

Crovetti, R., et al. "The Influence of Thermic Effect of Food on Satiety," *European Journal of Clinical Nutrition* vol. 52 (1998): 482–88.

Lemaitre, R. N., et al. "N-3 Polyunsaturated Fatty Acids, Fatal Ischemic Heart Disease, and Nonfatal Myocardial Infarction in Older Adults: The Cardiovascular Health Study," *American Journal of Clinical Nutrition* vol. 77 (2003): 279–80.

Robinson, S. M., et al. "Protein Turnover and Thermogenesis in Response to High-Protein and High-Carbohydrate Feeding in Men," *American Journal of Clinical Nutrition* vol. 52 (1990): 72–80.

Chapter 12

Allison, D. B., et al. "A Novel Soy-Based Meal Replacement Formula for Weight Loss among Obese Individuals: A Randomized Controlled Clinical Trial," *European Journal of Clinical Nutrition* vol. 57 (2003): 514–22.

Bell, J., and S. J. Whiting. "Elderly Women Need Dietary Protein to Maintain Bone Mass," *Nutrition Reviews* vol. 60 (10 Pt. 1) (2002): 337–41.

Boirie, Y., et al. "Slow and Fast Dietary Proteins Differently Modulate Postprandial Protein Accretion," *Proceedings of the National Academy of Science USA* vol. 94 (1997):14930–35.

Clare, D. A., and H. E. Swaisgood. "Bioactive Milk Peptides: A Prospectus," *Journal of Diary Science* vol. 83: 1187–95.

Erkkila, A. T., et al. "N-3 Fatty Acids and 5-Year Risks of Death and Cardiovascular Disease Events in Patients with Coronary Artery Disease," *American Journal of Clinical Nutrition* vol. 78, no. 1 (2003): 1–2.

"Fat Content Best Guide to Buying Ground Beef," *The Columbus Dispatch* (May 17, 2000), http://www.dispatch.com/news/food/food00/food0517/282614.html.

He, K., et al. "Fish Consumption and Risk of Stroke in Men," *Journal of the American Medical Association* vol. 288, no. 24 (Dec. 25, 2002): 3130–36.

Melanson, K., et al. "Weight Loss and Total Lipid Profile Changes in Overweight Women Consuming Beef or Chicken as the Primary Protein Source," *Nutrition* vol. 19 (2003): 409–14.

Poortmans, J. R., and O. Dellalieux. "Do Regular High Protein Diets Have Potential Risks on Kidney Function in Athletes?" *International Journal of Sport Nutrition and Exercise Metabolism* vol. 10, no. 1 (2000): L28–38.

Scott, L. W., et al. "Effects of Beef and Chicken Consumption on Plasma Lipid Levels in Hypercholesterolemic Men," *Archives of Internal Medicine* vol. 154 (1994): 1261–67.

Song, W. O., et al. "Nutritional Contribution of Eggs to American Diets," *Journal of the American College of Nutrition* vol. 19 (2000): 556S–562S.

Van Niekerk, P. J., et al. "The Nutritional Composition of South African Eggs," *South African Medical Journal* vol. 83 (1993): 842–46.

Chapter 13

Alper, C. M., and R. D. Mattes. "Peanut Consumption Improves Indices of Cardiovascular Disease Risk in Healthy Adults," *Journal of the American College of Nutrition* vol. 22 (2003): 133–41.

Bell, R. R., M. J. Spencer, and J. L. Sherriff. "Voluntary exercise and Monounsaturated Canola Oil Reduce Fat Gain in Mice Fed Diets High in Fat," *Journal of Nutrition* vol. 127 (1997): 2006–10.

Chen, H., et al. "Eicosapentanoic Acid Inhibits Hypoxia-Reoxygenation-Induced Injury by Attenuating Upregulation of MMP-1 in Adult Rat Myocytes," *Cardiovascular Research* vol. 59 (2003): 7–13.

Grimsgaard, S., et al. "Highly Purified Eicosapentanoic Acid and Docosahexanoic Acid in Humans Have Similar Triacylglyerol-Lowering Effects but

Divergent Effects on Serum Fatty Acids," *American Journal of Clinical Nutriton* vol. 66 (1997): 649–59.

Kamphuis, M. M., et al. "The Effect of Conjugated Linoleic Acid Supplementation after Weight Loss on Body Weight Regain, Body Composition, and Resting Metabolic Rate in Overweight Subjects," *International Journal of Obesity and Related Metabolic Disorders* vol. 27 (2003): 840–47.

Lichtenstein, A. H. "Dietary Fat and Cardiovascular Disease Risk: Quantity or Quality?" *Journal of Womens Health* vol. 12 (2003): 109–14.

Nagao, T., et al. "Dietary Diacylglycerol Suppresses Accumulation of Body Fat Compared to Triacylglycerol in Men in a Double-Blind Controlled Trial," *Journal of Nutrition* vol. 130 (2000): 792–97.

Raastad, T., et al. "Omega-3 Fatty Acid Supplementation Does Not Improve Maximal Aerobic Power, Anaerobic Threshold and Running Performance in Well-Trained Soccer Players," *Scandinavian Journal of Medicine and Science in Sports* vol. 7 (1997): 25–31.

Tagawa, T., et al. "Long-Term Treatment with Eicosapentanoic Acid Improves Exercise-Induced Vasodilation in Patients with Coronary Artery Disease, *Hypertension Research* vol. 25 (2002): 823–29.

Von Schacky, C. "The Role of Omega-3 Fatty Acids in Cardiovascular Disease," *Current Atherosclerosis Reports* vol. 5 (2003): 139–45.

Yamamoto, K., et al. "Long-Term Ingestion of Dietary Diacylglycerol Lowers Serum Triacyglycerol in Type II Diabetic Patients with Hypertriglyceridemia," *Journal of Nutrition* vol. 131 (2001): 3204–7.

Chapter 14

Burke, L. M., et al. "Carbohydrate Loading Failed to Improve 100-Km Cycling Performance in a Placebo-Controlled Trial," *Journal of Applied Physiology* vol. 88 (2000): 1284–90.

Hawley, J. A. "Carbohydrate Loading and Exercise Performance: An Update," *Sports Medicine* vol. 24 (1997): 73–81.

Liu, S., et al. "A Prospective Study of Dietary Glycemic Load, Carbohydrate Intake, and Risk of Coronary Heart Disease in U.S. Women," *American Journal of Clinical Nutriton* vol. 71 (2000): 1455–61.

Ludwig, D. S., et al. "High Glycemic Index Foods, Overeating, and Obesity," *Pediatrics* vol. 103 (1999): E26.

McArdle, W. D., et al. *Sports & Exercise Nutrition* (Baltimore: Lippincott Williams & Wilkins, 1999), 347–48.

Thomas, D. E., et al. "Carbohydrate Feeding before Exercise: Effect of Glycemic Index," *International Journal of Sports Medicine* vol. 112 (1991): 180–86.

Westman, E. C. "Is Dietary Carbohydrate Essential for Human Nutrition?" (Letter to the Editor), *American Journal of Clinical Nutriton* vol. 75 (2002): 951–53.

Chapter 15

Bounous, G., and P. Gold. "The Biological Activity of Undenatured Dietary Whey Proteins: Role of Glutathione," *Clinical and Investigative Medicine* vol. 14 (1991): 296–309.

Hemila, H. "Vitamin C and Common Cold Incidence: A Review of Studies with Subjects under Heavy Physical Stress," *International Journal of Sports Medicine*, vol. 17 (1996): 379–83.

Kreider, R. B., D. Hill, G. Horton, M. Downes, S. Smith, and B. Anders. "Effects of Carbohydrate Supplementation during Intense Training on Dietary Patterns, Psychological Status, and Performance," *International Journal of Sport Nutrition," vol. 5 (1995): 125–35.

Meydani, M., et al. "Muscle Uptake of Vitamin E and Its Association with Muscle Fiber Type," *Journal of Nutritional Biochemistry* vol. 8, no. 2 (1997): 74–78.

Roy, B. D., et al. "The Influence of Post-Exercise Macronutrient Intake on Energy Balance and Protein Metabolism in Active Females Participating in Endurance Training," *International Journal of Sports Nutrition and Exercise Metabolism* vol. 12 (2002): 172–88.

Tipton, K. D., et al. "Timing of Amino Acid-Carbohydrate Ingestion Alters Anabolic Response of Muscle to Resistance Exercise," *American Journal of Physiology*, vol. 281 (2001): E197–E206.

Williams, M. B., et al. "Effects of Recovery Beverages on Glycogen Restoration and Endurance Exercise Performance," *Journal of Strength and Conditioning Research* vol. 17 (2003): 12–19.

Yaspelkis, B. B., III, J. G. Patterson, P. A. Anderla, Z. Ding, and J. L. Ivy. "Carbohydrate Supplementation Spares Muscle Glycogen during Variable-Intensity Exercise," *Journal of Applied Physiology* vol. 75 (1993): 1477–85.

Chapter 16

Bilz, S., et al. "Effects of Hypoosmolality on Whole-Body Lipolysis in Man," *Metabolism* vol. 48, no. 4 (1999): 472–76.

Febbraio, M., et al. "Effects of Carbohydrate Ingestion before and during Exercise on Glucose Kinetics and Performance," *Journal of Applied Physiology*, vol. 89 (2000): 2220–26.

Frank, M. S. B., M. C. Nahata, and M. H. Hilty. "Glycerol: A Review of Its Pharmacology, Pharmacokinetics, Adverse Reactions, and Clinical Use," *Pharmacotherapy* vol. 1 (1981): 147–60.

Grandjean, A. C., et al. "The Effect of Caffeinated, Non-Caffeinated, Caloric and Non-Caloric Beverages on Hydration," *Journal of the American College of Nutrition* vol. 19 (2000): 591–600.

Montner, P., et al. "Pre-Exercise Glycerol Hydration Improves Cycling Endurance Time." *International Journal of Sports Medicine* vol. 17, no. 1 (1996): 27–33.

Wagner, D. R. "Hyperhydrating with Glycerol: Implications for Athletic Performance," *Journal of the American Dietetic Association* vol. 99 (1999): 207–12.

Wemple, R. D., et al. "Caffeine and Caffeine-Free Sports Drinks: Effects on Urine Production at Rest and during Prolonged Exercise," *International Journal of Sports Medicine* vol. 18 (1997): 40–46.

Chapter 17

Antonio, J., et al. "The Effects of Bovine Colostrum Supplementation on Body Composition and Exercise Performance in Active Men and Women," *Nutrition* vol. 17 (2001): 243–47.

Buckley, J. D., et al. "Bovine Colostrum Supplementation during Endurance Running Training Improves Recovery, but not Performance," *Journal of Science and Medicine in Sport* vol. 5 (2002): 65–79.

Buckley, J. D., et al. "Effect of Bovine Colostrum on Anaerobic Exercise Performance and Plasma Insulin-Like Growth Factor 1," *Journal of Sports Science* vol. 21 (2003): 577–88.

Coombes, J. S., et al. "Dose Effects of Oral Bovine Colostrum on Physical Work Capacity in Cyclists," *Medicine and Science in Sports and Exercise* vol. 34 (2002): 1184–88.

Fiorotto, M., et al. "Colostrum Feeding Increases Myosin Heavy Chain (MHC) mRNA Abundance in Skeletal Muscle of Newborn Piglets," *Experimental Biology* (1999) A53(72.1).

Fletcher, R. H., and K. M. Fairfield. "Vitamins for Chronic Disease Prevention in Adults: Clinical Applications," *Journal of the American Medical Association* vol. 287, no. 23 (June 19, 2000): 3127–29.

Stray-Gundersen, J., et al. "Living High-Training Low: Altitude Training Improves Sea Level Performance in Male and Female Elite Runners," *Journal of Applied Physiology* vol. 91 (2001): 1113–20.

Williams, M. B., et al. "Effects of Recovery Beverages on Glycogen Restoration and Endurance Exercise Performance," *Journal of Strength and Conditioning Research* vol. 17 (2003): 12–19.

Williams, M. H. *The Ergogenics Edge* (Champaign, IL: Human Kinetics, 1998).

Zemel, M. B. "Role of Dietary Calcium and Dairy Products in Modulating Adiposity," *Lipids* vol. 38 (2003): 139–46.

Chapter 18

Brehm, B. J., et al. "A Randomized Trial Comparing a Very Low Carbohydrate Diet and a Calorie-Restricted Low Fat Diet on Body Weight and Cardiovascular Risk Factors in Healthy Women," *Journal of Clinical Endocrinology and Metabolism* vol. 88 (April 2003): 1617–23.

Layman, D. K., et al. "Increased Dietary Protein Modifies Glucose and Insulin Homeostasis in Adult Women during Weight Loss," *Journal of Nutrition* vol. 133 (2003): 405–10.

Layman, D. K., et al. "A Reduced Ratio of Dietary Carbohydrate to Protein Improves Body Composition and Blood Lipid Profiles during Weight Loss in Adult Women," *Journal of Nutrition* vol. 133 (Feb. 2003): 411–17.

Melanson, E., et al. "Relation between Calcium Intake and Fat Oxidation in Adult Humans," *International Journal of Obesity* vol. 27 (2003): 196–203.

Parker, B., et al. "Effect of a High-Protein, High-Monounsaturated Fat Weight Loss Diet on Glycemic Control and Lipid Levels in Type 2 Diabetes," *Diabetes Care* vol. 25 (2002): 425–30.

Piatti, P. M., et al. "Hypocaloric High-Protein Diet Improves Glucose Oxidation and Spares Lean Body Mass: Comparison of Hypocaloric High-Carbohydrate Diet," *Metabolism* vol. 43 (Dec. 1994): 1481–87.

Skov, A. R., et al. "Randomized Trial on Protein vs Carbohydrate in Ad Libitum Fat Reduced Diet for the Treatment of Obesity," *International Journal of Obesity and Related Metabolic Disorders* vol. 23 (May 1999): 528–36.

Volek, J. S., et al. "Body Composition and Hormonal Responses to a Carbohydrate-Restricted Diet," *Metabolism* vol. 51 (2002): 864–70.

Volek, J. S., and E. C. Westman. "Very Low Carbohydrate Weight Loss Diets Revisited," *Cleveland Journal of Medicine* vol. 69, no. 11 (2002): 849–62.

Chapter 19

Hickson, R. C., et al. "Potential for Strength and Endurance Training to Amplify Endurance Performance," *Journal of Applied Physiology* vol. 65 (1988): 2285–90.

Marcinik, E. J., et al. "Effects of Strength Training on Lactate Threshold and Endurance Performance," *Medicine and Science in Sports and Exercise* vol. 23 (1991): 739–43.

Paavolainen, L., et al. "Explosive-Strength Training Improves 5-Km Running Time by Improving Running Economy and Muscle Power," *Journal of Applied Physiology* vol. 5 (1986): 1527–33.

Palmer, C. D., and G. G. Sleivert. "Running Economy Is Impaired following a Single Bout of Resistance Exercise," *Journal of Science and Medicine in Sport* vol. 4 (2001): 447–593.

White, L. J., et al. "Effectiveness of Cycle Cross-Training between Competitive Seasons in Female Distance Runners," *Journal of Strength and Conditioning Research* vol. 17 (2003): 319–23.

Wilber, R. I., et al. "Influence of Water Run Training on the Maintenance of Aerobic Performance," *Medicine and Science in Sports and Exercise* vol. 28 (1996): 1056–62.

Index

H

I